NANTUCKET
Then and Now

BEING AN UPDATED HISTORY AND GUIDE

By Winston Williams

Illustrated with photographs by the author

DODD, MEAD & COMPANY
New York

Picture Credits

The photographs on pages 51, 56, 59 are used by permission and through the courtesy of Mystic Seaport, Inc., Mystic, Connecticut. The one on page 101 (bottom) is by Pedro Aquacasa. Those of the freeze-up on page 109 are by Rollin Manville. Clinton Folger's horse-drawn car on page 120 is used through the courtesy of Mr. and Mrs. George Pinault. All other photographs are by the author. The maps on pages 40 and 113 are by Dyno Lowenstein.

Copyright © 1977 by Winston Williams
All rights reserved
No part of this book may be reproduced in any form
without permission in writing from the publisher
Printed in the United States of America

1   2   3   4   5   6   7   8   9   10

Library of Congress Cataloging in Publication Data

Williams, Winston.
        Nantucket then and now, being an updated history
and guide.

        Includes index.
        SUMMARY: A history of an island off the coast of
Massachusetts with particular emphasis on its long
involvement with the whaling industry.
        1.   Nantucket, Mass.—History—Juvenile literature.
2.   Whaling—Massachusetts—Nantucket—Juvenile litera-
ture.   [1.   Nantucket, Mass.—History.   2.   Whaling—
Massachusetts—Nantucket]   I.   Title.
F72.N2W54   974.4'97   76-50543
ISBN 0-396-07411-1

This book is dedicated to
the Nantucketer
—and also to my late friend, Bill Daly

 Acknowledgments

I AM most grateful to Tom and Marie Giffin of Nantucket's newspaper, *The Inquirer and Mirror*, who helped me in a number of ways to research and write this book. Their cooperation was invaluable.

I would also like to express my appreciation to The Camera Shop, namely Gene Mahon, Lee Dunn, and Judson Camp, whose excellent work on my photographic prints impressed me as well as my editor.

In addition I would like to thank Edouard Stackpole, the island's prominent historian, for his assistance during my researches, and Barbara Andrews, Byron Coffin, and Rollin Manville, all of whom aided me in checking historical facts and figures. And special thanks to Albert Louer of Mystic Seaport, Inc.

In a variety of ways I have gained help from my father and mother, Mr. and Mrs. Donald Williams, Mr. and Mrs. George Pinault, Roger Young, William Shaw, Matthew Jaeckle, Mimi Haskell, Killen Real Estate, and the Nantucket Steamship Authority.

My thanks also to that couple who allowed me to quote from the log of the *Mary Mitchell*. For reasons of their own, they chose to remain nameless.

Finally, I would like to express sincerely my appreciation to Joe Ann Daly, my editor. Without her aid and understanding this book would never have been written.

—WINSTON WILLIAMS

# Contents

1. The Island Pilgrims   13
2. The Birth of Whaling   30
3. A War and a Whaleship   42
4. The Golden Age   55
5. At the Home Port End   69
6. The End of an Era   84
7. The Trend Toward Tourism   98
8. Of Trains and Autos   112
9. Modern-day Nantucket   124
    Index   137

NANTUCKET
Then and Now

The Macy House at 99 Main Street. Hundreds of tourists visit this land-mark each summer.

1

The Island Pilgrims

Nantucket island is located approximately thirty miles at sea off the coast of Massachusetts. From east to west it measures fifteen miles long and its average width, north and south, is three and a half miles, having a total land area of 30,000 acres. Remotely shaped like a strutting swan, the island's geological birth is similar to other East Coast islands such as Martha's Vineyard and Block Island—a clump of sand and soil left by the huge glaciers of the Ice Age.

Affectionately called "The Little Grey Lady of the Sea" by her ancestral inhabitants, Nantucket's quaint charm attracts thousands upon thousands of tourists each summer. They flock to the island's fifty-four miles of white beaches and to its cobwebbed network of twisting, narrow lanes of the town where historic landmarks and old houses seem to lurk around every corner.

Statistics tell the story of Nantucket's magical appeal. Recent figures of the Steamship Authority, which runs five boats daily from Cape Cod to Nantucket, show that between June 15 and September 14 the line transported 101,850 passengers and 9,666 cars to the island. These figures do not include a competitive boat line which makes five trips a day, nor the countless flights by Air New England and smaller air outfits, or the huge flotilla of visiting yachts which fill the harbor and tie up at the hundreds of slips around the waterfront piers. Indeed it would be a conservative guess that, during the summer season, at least a half million people visit the island.

But statistics, though revealing, are dull. One has to come to Nantucket oneself to experience and understand this appeal. One has to see for oneself the old, worn cobblestones of Main Street, the turning and creaking vanes of the Old Mill on Prospect Hill, and the rolling moors of Saul's Hills which strikingly resemble the heathlands of Scotland. One might even notice the total absence of traffic lights, billboards, and the usual national hotel and restaurant chains. Not only that, one would be hard pressed to find the usual hot dog stands, cheap motels, and other honky-tonk establishments which clutter the beachsides of other resorts. There simply are not any. The fact is, Nantucket is one of the few places in the country that can boast the absence of such things.

Most people, after their initial visit to this remarkable island, will come back at some point; and not just once, but time after time again. It is as if the island's magical charm acts like a benevolent, chronic disease which gets into one's blood, and never disappears. There is no known cure for Nantucket's spell.

The more one becomes familiar with Nantucket, the more one

An armada of bicycles whose owners and renters have left temporarily to have lunch at a popular restaurant.

14

wonders about her settlers hundreds of years ago. Who were they? What were they like? What was the island like? It's hard to answer these questions with 100 percent authority. During the first fifty years of colonization, only scattered records were kept and then some of the few facts which do exist sometimes conflict. To describe these beginning years, a writer is forced to depend almost as much on his imagination and instinct as on the handful of facts. But there is enough known to put the puzzle together. Suffice it to say, Nantucket's history is intriguing and riddled with adventure, enormous prosperity, and world recognition. It is also marked by periods of terrible poverty, suffering, and tragedy.

The discovery of Nantucket is credited to an Englishman named Bartholomew Gosnold. The year was 1602 and, with a company of others, he was on a voyage to Virginia where he hoped to start a plantation. Little has been recorded about this event save for the fact it was the high bluffs of Sankaty which he first sighted. Because of the beauty of these sandy cliffs which line the eastern shore of the island and the probability that Gosnold had been at sea for a long time, one could assume he was tempted to land. But he never did. There could have been a number of reasons why. Bad weather could have been a factor. Or, seeing the white water of the rips and shoals off Siasconset to the south, he gave the island a wide berth, preferring discretion to shipwreck. Or he might have sailed offshore around the rips and then closed the land again along the south shore, only to find no opening or harbor.

Another interesting deterrent is plausible. It has been estimated that in the early 1600s, at least 1,000 Indians lived on the island. The sight of Gosnold's ship could have caused excited

The cliffs of Sankaty Head, Gosnold's first sight of Nantucket in 1602.

curiosity and perhaps hundreds lined the tops of the bluffs to watch. One can imagine that this could have presented an awesome and intimidating scene for Gosnold and his group. Whatever the reasons may have been, it must have been a bitter pill to swallow when the Englishman made the decision to bear away for Virginia, knowing that he and his charges would be facing an additional week or two at sea.

It wasn't until fifty-seven years later, in the fall of 1659, that white men first stepped foot on Nantucket soil. Because he had committed a "crime" against his religion earlier in the year, Thomas Macy and his family, along with his friend Edward Starbuck, abandoned their homes in Salisbury, Massachusetts. Braving the elements in an open boat, they sailed around the backside of Cape Cod, eventually landing on the western end of Nantucket at Madaket where they spent their first winter in the area of what is now known as Hither Creek.

Madaket Harbor to the left and Hither Creek to the right. It was this area where Thomas Macy and his group spent the first winter in 1659.

Just a few facts demonstrate the stubborn pioneering spirit Thomas Macy must have had. It is known he fled his homeland England and migrated to Salisbury in 1640 in search of religious freedom. According to *History of Nantucket*, written by Obed Macy, a relative, in 1835, "he lived here [Salisbury] in good repute for twenty years, where he acquired a good interest, consisting of a tract of land 1,000 acres, a good house, and considerable stock." Even in those days, this was substantial wealth. The significant point here was that Thomas Macy was willing to give all this up, burn his bridges, and migrate to Nantucket *for the same reason* he had fled England twenty years before—a strong-willed disbelief in and hatred of religious persecution. (Purportedly his "crime" in Salisbury had been the kindness to allow a few wandering Quakers to seek shelter in his home during a rain storm. Shortly afterward, as news spread around, he received a reprimand from the town officials in the form of a letter.)

Migrating to Nantucket, although a mere fifty miles instead of across the Atlantic Ocean, must have conjured up many dangers in Thomas Macy's mind. He did not know whether the soil could be cultivated. He did not know if there would be enough game, if any, to sustain them. About the only thing he did know was that there were Indians living there and, if they turned out to be hostile, he had no avenue of retreat.

Macy and his group must have had extraordinarily strong characters. It is enough, because of conviction and belief, that a man be forced to uproot his home and its security once in his life. Thomas Macy had the fortitude to do it twice, not having the slightest idea what Nantucket had in store for him and his companions.

Fortunately things turned out well. "They found the island covered with wood," wrote Obed Macy in his *History of Nantucket*, "and inhabited by Indians, who depended for subsistence

Site of Tristram Coffin's home at Sherburne. The present Madaket Road lies a mere two hundred yards from this monument.

on fishing, fouling and hunting. Game was remarkably plenty, and continued so many years afterward; and the adjacent shores and waters abounded with many kinds of fish. Here they spent the winter, a single family, confined on an island among native Indians of whose character and language they were almost entirely ignorant."

That first winter in Madaket passed uneventfully. The white settlers' relations with the Indians must have gone well because in the following summer of 1660, Edward Starbuck returned to Salisbury and brought back with him ten new families who planned to settle on Nantucket permanently.

It is one of those quirks of history that Nantucket's ownership, as far as the white man was concerned at least, was determined years before Macy and Starbuck set foot on Madaket for the first

20

time in 1659. Originally, Thomas Mayhew had purchased the island from William, Earl of Sterling, in 1641. Then, only months prior to Macy's and Starbuck's voyage, Mayhew sold Nantucket to nine others in equal shares, keeping one for himself, which is the land area now known as Quaise on the south shore of the inner harbor. Among these "Original Nine Purchasers" was Tristram Coffin, Sr., who was the leader and originator of the transaction. One can still see the monument which marks the site of his house on a hill a few miles west of town, overlooking a pond and Nantucket Sound to the north. The others in this group were Thomas Macy, Christopher Hussey, Richard Swain, Thomas Barnard, Peter Coffin, Stephen Greenleaf, John Swain, and William Pile. In addition, to help settle the island, each of these nine selected an associate so that, in the end, there were twenty original purchasers. It is interesting to note that twelve family names of these original twenty can still be found in Nantucket's current telephone book.

It is said that many of these original purchasers came from the Salisbury area, so one must assume that among the ten families which came back to the island with Edward Starbuck in the summer of 1660, some, if not all, were these owners.

After a few years, the settlers abandoned Madaket and a new site was established near the north shore in the area immediately adjacent to Maxcy's and Capaum ponds, about two miles west of the present town. With its rolling hills, this new site offered more shelter in the winter and cooling breezes in the summer. At the time, Capaum Pond had a cut which opened to Nantucket Sound, making it a suitable harbor. There was also a good spring in the area. The new settlement was officially incorporated in 1671. Two years later it was given the name of Sherburne by the Governor of New York, the island being under that province's jurisdiction at the time.

Capaum Pond originally opened into Nantucket Sound and served as a small harbor during the Sherburne days. Its entrance long since closed up by a storm, it now is a quiet pond, seen by any who choose to swim off the beach at Dionis on the north shore.

For three decades Sherburne grew and flourished. The settlers maintained their livelihood by farming, raising stock, and fishing. According to historian Obed Macy, a good understanding grew between the settlers and the Indians. The latter were willing to work if they were given just pay, and were ready to sell their land so long as the settlers gave them a good price. ". . . the whites never presumed privileges which they had not fairly paid for," wrote Macy. In every case, when there was a land transaction between an Indian and a white, not only was a deed drawn up and payment made, but also the Indian was given certain rights to the land he had sold to help support his family whenever necessary. (For some reason during the early years of Sherburne, all deeds and records were sent and stored in a house in Salisbury.

Eventually the house burned down and, with it, the documents. This is one reason Nantucket's early history is so difficult to trace.)

These dealings with the Indians give us additional insight into the character of the first Nantucketers. The settlers' regard for them indicated their justness, sense of fair play, and an apparent lack of any feelings of superiority. At heart the settlers were clearly pacifists. Some would say they treated the Indians kindly because they were greatly outnumbered and feared massacre. Yet in later years, when the coin had turned and the whites outnumbered the Indians, the good relationship remained steadfast.

The plight of the Nantucket Indian was similar to many of the other tribes throughout the country. When Macy and Starbuck first came in 1659, there were great numbers. When the settlers began local whaling, an activity they had no idea would make Nantucket and Nantucketers famous in the future, the Indians were allowed to participate and even held such honored positions as steerers and harpooners. Indeed, it is logical to reason that the Indians went whaling long before the settlers came and, in many cases, taught the settlers to a certain extent.

But daily contact with the whites exposed them to diseases their bodies could not tolerate, even the common cold. As a result, their population declined swiftly. To add to this, they developed a warm affection for the whites' alcohol and, when not busy farming or fishing, were usually drunk. This didn't add to their health either. Many, too, were lost on whaling ventures.

Thus the painful figures of a vanished race. Just a little more than a century after that first winter in 1659, only 358 Indians were left. Then, in 1764, as if history had no compassion, a tragic epidemic swept the island, killing 222 out of the remainng 358. The last known Indian to die on Nantucket was Abram Quary in 1854, and he was, at that, not full-blooded. It seems that the only wrong the Nantucket Indians did to create their own demise was to adapt to the white man's ways.

But to return to early Sherburne years, the settlers must have met with relative success in farming because in 1666, the first windmill was built at Wesco Pond, now located near Lily Street in the heart of the present town. Peter Folger, an inhabitant of Martha's Vineyard, was asked to move to Nantucket and become the official Town Miller. He must have been a talented man, for in addition to his duties as miller, he also took on the responsibilities of weaver and interpreter of the Indian language, which he spoke well. He was also to become the grandfather of Benjamin Franklin. (His colleague, Thomas Macy, would have a famous relative in the future too—the Macy who founded the famous department store of that name in New York City.)

By 1676 the white population had increased substantially and other settlements made their appearances in different sectors of the island. Siasconset and Sesachacha villages were built on the east coast of the island to take advantage of the great numbers of codfish which abounded there. As local whaling began to develop, whale houses were constructed at Miacomet on the south shore, as well as fishing stages (crude overnight shelters for fishermen) at Quidnet just north of Sesachacha village and Weeweeder on the south shore, now called Surfside. But the main populace remained at Sherburne around Capaum and Maxcy's ponds.

Over the last thirty years of the century, however, a slow but steady exodus was made toward the east to what is the site of the present town where the larger inner harbor offered better facilities. Evidence of this exodus starts as far back as the first mill built in 1666 and operated by Peter Folger. The mill was a water mill and Wesco Pond offered one of the only running water streams on the island. (Unfortunately, this mill has long since

24

The Jethro Coffin House, oldest structure on the island, built in 1686. Note the cobblestones and old well in foreground.

West Chester Street of yesteryear. Starting near the area of Maxcy's Pond, it winds eastward over the moors. In the earliest days, it served as the only route connecting the original settlement of Sherburne to the present site of Nantucket town.

West Chester Street of today, showing its ending in Nantucket town after meandering three miles through the moors.

been torn down, but the pond, now a creek, can still be seen in the hollow on the north side of Lily Street.) More evidence is the location of the "Oldest House"—the Jethro Coffin House which still stands where it was originally built in 1686 on Sunset Hill, an elevated knoll in the northwest section of the present town.

This gravitation toward the harbor created a connecting road linking the old site to the new one. Today it is called West Chester Street and is Nantucket's oldest road. In town it starts very near where Peter Folger's mill at Wesco Pond once stood. If one wishes to take an unhurried, two-mile walk back into history, all one has to do is take the route along West Chester. Going first through an attractive part of town, it turns westward and passes Sunset Hill and the Jethro Coffin House on the right. When it reaches the town's outskirts, it turns into a sand road. Soon there are no houses as it continues toward the empty moors. For perhaps half a mile on, it winds up and down, to and fro, gradually becoming less distinct. Finally it reaches a hilltop overlooking Maxcy's Pond. Here, posed conspicuously, is a stone monument which not only commemorates the original site of Sherburne but also marks the spot where the first meetinghouse stood. That meetinghouse is still in use today and is the vestry wing of the Old North Church on Centre Street, one of the town's main arteries which originates from Main Street.

It is a pleasant spot, this hilltop. One can observe Nantucket Sound to the north and all the hills and valleys which were within the perimeter of the original Sherburne. It is easy in this quiet place to imagine just which slope Thomas Macy selected for his cornfield, which valley Edward Starbuck chose to build his house, and where Tristram Coffin decided to pasture his stock.

But it's all academic now and has been as far back as 1700, for that year marked the real beginning of the end for the original Sherburne site. A vicious storm closed the opening to Capaum

Harbor, making it the quiet pond it is today. From that time on, the main settlement steadily relocated itself to the present town site and was still called Sherburne until 1795 when the name was changed to Nantucket.

If there was any one year during those early decades which had a profound effect on Nantucket's destiny in the future, it would probably have to be 1673. It was during this year that the settlers first began searching and killing the local whales in the small boats. Unknown to them at the time, this was the birth of an industry which would, in the years to come, proclaim Nantucket as its capital and send Nantucketers to practically every conceivable corner of the globe.

The Old North Church on Centre Street. Its present vestry wing is the old meetinghouse of Sherburne, built in the 1660s

 2

The Birth of Whaling

Most sources tell us that local whaling offshore was begun by Nantucketers in 1673. What could have been one of the primary factors which precipitated this, however, was the first whaling "expedition" the previous year. There are no clear-cut records which prove this venture ever happened. Rather, as one historian has put it, the proof of this particular happening was handed down by tradition, as one generation told the next through the years. But even if the source is only by word of mouth, it is hard to disregard it completely. Something, at least, of a similar nature must have happened to create enough excitement for the sudden interest in whales the following year.

Be that as it may, sometime in 1672, a whale found its way into the inner harbor and remained several days. Its presence caused considerable excitement and apparently some of the original purchasers tried to prevent it from getting back out into the Sound. It is not mentioned how this was done, but an educated

A look to the west from Pocomo Head, showing the inner harbor and Nantucket town in the background.

guess was that Coffin, Macy, Starbuck and the others used their small boats and "herded" the whale into shoal water. Whatever method was used, and while they were busy using it, others ashore built a crude harpoon and the whale was ultimately killed, hauled up on the beach, then cut up and boiled.

This incident must have fired up the imagination of the settlers, for we do have records that the town commissioned a man named James Lopar, who lived on the Cape, to teach them about whales and whale processing. In those early days, it was known that the Cape Codders were much more advanced in the art of local whaling than anyone else. A document was drawn up and read in part: "5th 4th mo. 1672 James Lopar doth Ingage to carry on a design of Whale Citching on the Island of Nantucket, that is the said James Ingage to be a third in all respeekes, and som of the Town Ingage Also to carrey on the other two thirds with him in like manner etc."

No one knows whether this agreement between the town and Lopar was successful. But the continued and increasing pursuit of local whales in the following years indicates that it most likely did. At the same time, a man named John Savage was invited to be cooper, a carpenter who made casks to hold whale oil, the settlers offering him ten acres of land, three cows, and a horse as inducements.

So in 1673, the settlers seriously started to involve themselves in a local whaling industry. There was certainly no lack for whales around the island. Numerous accounts establish their abundance locally in the late 1600s, one of the most poignant being Obed Macy's description of a group of Nantucketers watching a pod of whales north of Quidnet off the east shore in 1690: ". . . some persons were on a high hill, afterwards called Folly House Hill, observing the whales spouting and sporting with each other, when one observed, 'there,' pointing to the sea, 'is the green pasture where our childrens' grandchildren will go for bread.'" How great a prophet that person turned out to be!

Again in 1690, the town commissioned another Cape Codder named Ichabod Paddock to help the Nantucketers learn the most efficient way to kill whales and extract their oil. Soon after, whaling became the principal industry of the island. The Indians participated as whalemen too, and it was because of them that the Nantucketers were able to send out many more boats than had they gone out by themselves.

For the first forty years or so of local whaling, the Nantucketers used small open boats from which they harpooned the whales. (Most of the creatures found around the island were of the right whale species.) These boats were generally rowed, and later masts were stepped, enabling the whalemen to climb aloft and gain a superior vantage point to observe. Also outposts were

32

The Whaling Museum on lower Broad Street. In the past this building served as both a candle factory and a warehouse.

erected on the bluffs along the south and east shores and watches constantly kept.

Once a whale was harpooned and subdued, it was towed ashore and "saved." This was merely the process of peeling the blubber off the whale with the aid of a "crab," an implement very much like a ship's capstan or winch, which hauled the blubber off as it was cut. The blubber was then stowed aboard a horse-drawn buggy and taken to the try house where it was boiled, or "tried out," in big try pots in order to extract the oil. (These try pots are now on display at the Whaling Museum near the Steamboat Wharf.) In some cases these try houses were very near the town homes, and one can imagine the almost overwhelming stench which must have permeated the town when the wind was in the wrong direction. In future years, when the large whaling vessels were used, the town would be spared from this smell because whales would be processed on the spot aboard ship during the long three- and four-year voyages to the Pacific. But in these early years, living in town at times must have been suffocating, especially in the year 1726 when eighty-six whales were killed and processed ashore.

During the first two decades of 1700, certain changes and events took place which helped the island prosper more. In this period, the small open boats were gradually replaced by larger sloops whose average size was 35 tons. Records show, for instance, that in 1715, six of these vessels grossed a sum total of $4,888.88 worth of whale oil. But the event that would ultimately redirect the destiny of the industry happened three years earlier in 1712. Cruising the island's south shore in search of right whales, Captain Christopher Hussey's sloop was suddenly struck by an unexpected northerly gale which drove him far out to sea. Quite by accident, he ran into a pod of sperm whales. Killing one, he returned to the island, bringing ashore Nantucket's first sperm whale. (Years before a dead sperm whale did wash ashore. But Hussey's was the first that was "taken" on an actual expedition.)

Hussey's catch produced two related effects. First, when it was discovered that Hussey's sperm whale possessed a much finer and more valuable oil, Nantucketers in the future would give priority to the sperm rather than the right whale. Secondly, because the sperm whale's habitat was much farther offshore, whalemen started making longer voyages to the "deep" or "southwards" in search of them. And this, in turn, necessitated larger vessels.

Resultingly, the size of the whaling vessels grew dramatically. Thirty- to 40-ton sloops began probing the "deep" off the south shore. Their voyages lasted a month or more and, when they killed a whale, they returned home where it was processed. Then the same ships were sent out again immediately. Later, sloops and schooners were put into service, their tonnage increasing to

Commercial fishing craft tied up at the Straight Wharf today.

50 tons average. As whales near the island became scarcer, new vessels were commissioned, these in the 70-ton class so that they could make longer trips to the east of the Grand Banks. During the winters, all vessels were hauled up on the beaches, presumably in the harbor, and lashed securely side by side in case of storms.

Because of the growing whaling activity, the first town wharf, now Straight Wharf, was built by Richard Macy in 1723. (Richard was the grandson of Thomas Macy, who died in April of 1682 at the age of seventy-four.) Warehouses were constructed south of Straight Wharf to store whaling equipment and new try houses were built to the south of the warehouses. The white population had swelled to well over 700 as the industry created many jobs for coopers, carpenters, riggers, and blacksmiths as well as a variety of positions aboard the vessels themselves.

The year 1745 was a banner one for the expansion of Nantucket's whaling industry. It was during this year that the island sent its first vessel directly to England where it sold its cargo of whale oil. Prior to this, Boston had been the island's main market. Boston whalemen reloaded their own vessels with the purchased Nantucket oil and sailed to England themselves, making a fine profit. Because of this, word got around in England and the European continent that Nantucket oil was top quality. At the same time, Nantucket shipowners and captains felt that Boston wasn't giving them a fair price for their oil. So in 1745 they demonstrated their displeasure with the Bostonian businessmen and simply sailed their own island ship directly to Great Britain.

The voyage, profitwise, turned out to be a successful one with unexpected fringe benefits. Besides offering a good price for the ship's oil, the British also sold the Nantucket captain hemp, hardware, and sail cloth at a much cheaper price than Boston had ever offered. This marked the beginning of a long business partnership between England and Nantucket, and an increasing number of island vessels sailed directly across the Atlantic year after year.

In the following decades, Nantucket ships started making longer trips to the Gulf of St. Lawrence, the Caribbean, the Western Islands (the Azores and Cape Verde Islands) and even to the coast of Brazil in search of the sperm whale. And, eventually, at some point in the 1700s, whale oil processing was done almost exclusively aboard the ships themselves. Quite a far cry from the days of Christopher Hussey and the local whaling in open boats before him.

By the 1760s, Nantucket was prospering. In 1762, for instance, the island's fleet increased to seventy-eight vessels which brought in 9,440 barrels of whale oil. In 1765, the fleet had increased to 101, bringing in 11,512 barrels, and in 1768 there were 125 ships which brought in 15,439. As has been said, some of this oil was sold to the English, but there were other markets as well. With this prosperity, the population boomed, and in 1764 there were 3,220 whites living on the island. The enormity of these figures can be fully appreciated if one remembers it was a little more than one hundred years before that the intrepid Thomas Macy group spent their first winter at Madaket.

During these first seventy years of the eighteenth century, things were happening ashore too. Brant Point, one of the oldest lighthouses in the country, was built with public funds in 1746. Its location was where it is today—on a point opposite the town where the outer channel runs into the inner harbor. Today, the steamers and ferries round this same old point on their way to the town piers. In that same year of 1746, the "Old Mill" was constructed and still grinds corn on Prospect Hill which overlooks the town. By now the town was completely settled at its present

site and house construction flourished. The town purchased its first fire engine in 1750 and a second one twelve years later. Old South Wharf was built in 1760, and in 1769, at the very tip of the long, narrow peninsula which extends to the north on the east side of the island, Great Point lighthouse was erected.

What were the Nantucketers like in those days? Our early historian Obed Macy wrote, "The inhabitants, generally, were attached to their place of nativity and were seldom desirous of leaving it. They were so closely connected by birth, similarity of pursuits, and habits of intimacy, that in some respects they appeared and conducted as one family. Perhaps, there is not another place in the world of equal magnitude, where the inhabitants were so closely connected by consanguinity as in this, which added much to the harmony of the people and their attachment to the place." He goes on to say, "When strangers came to the island, the longer they stayed, the more they were pleased with the people, their manners and customs: coming with no intention of the kind, they often formed matrimonial engagements and became inhabitants . . ."

Macy's reference to strangers coming to the island and their reaction to it only proves that Nantucket's magical appeal referred to in the first chapter has been around for a long, long time.

The character and habits of the Nantucketer in the middle of the eighteenth century were greatly influenced by Quakerism. Yet this isn't a surprise. Although the original twenty purchasers were Baptists and Presbyterians, we have already learned that Thomas Macy was sympathetic with the Quakers during his last

Brant Point lighthouse, built in 1746, is reputably the oldest lighthouse in the United States. For more than two centuries, it has guided ships from the channel around to the inner harbor and docks.

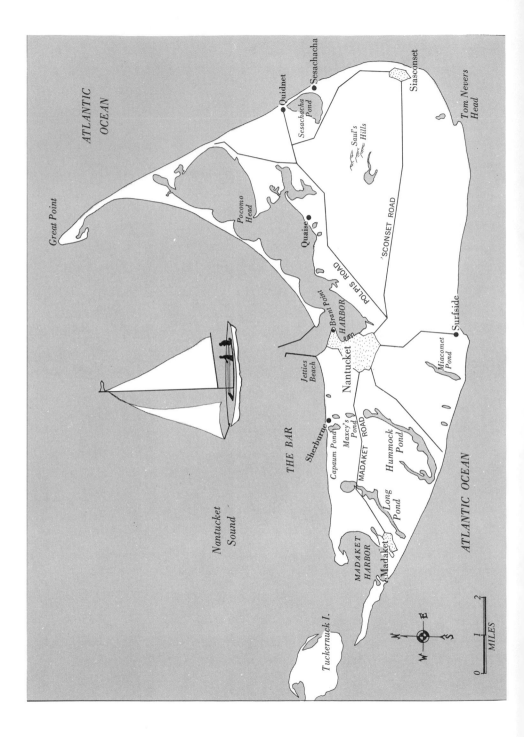

year in Salisbury. We have also seen how justly the settlers dealt with the Indians. Finally, life in the earlier years on the island was simple, characterized by hard work and the natural situation to help and share with one's neighbor. In a sense, then, the early settlers' outlooks on life were compatible to Quaker philosophy. So when a Quaker named Thomas Story came to Nantucket around 1704, he found it comparatively easy to convert the islanders to Quakerism. Because of his visit, Nantucket's first Society of Friends was established in 1708 and, for the next 150 years or so, the religion played a dominating role in the island community.

And so was the state of Nantucket and its people in the early 1770s. As a united group of extraordinary folk, they had managed to settle an island, live hospitably and in harmony with the Indians, and build up a whaling industry which was likely the most prosperous of its kind anywhere in the world, sending Nantucketers as far afield as the coast of Brazil and the Azores. And Nantucket's fleet had grown to 150 vessels, many of which were now square-riggers.

But terrible privation and suffering for the little island and its people were in the offing, for the Revolution was about to erupt. For the duration of this war, Nantucket would be literally cut off from the world and would find herself her own prisoner.

3

A War and a Whaleship

A<small>T</small> the outbreak of the Revolution, Nantucket's thriving whaling industry came to an abrupt halt. Because of the increasing presence of British warships and privateers, the island's more than 150 vessels, representing almost 15,000 tons, became immobilized and useless. Of course some of this fleet was still at sea at the beginning of hostilities, but it is impossible to determine the exact number and how many of these safely managed to return to port. But one can reasonably assume that during those critical months of 1775 after the Battle of Lexington, at least a hundred sloops, schooners, brigs, and other square-riggers were either anchored in the harbor or tied up to Straight Wharf and Old South Wharf side by side. For the most part abandoned because of their uselessness, their spars, rigging, and hulls began the slow process of decay.

At the outset of the war, the island population had grown to 4,500. Some families, in fear the island would be sacked by the

With her maze of yards and rigging, the newly built brig Unicorn's outline might give one a little indication of what Nantucket's waterfront looked like two hundred years ago.

British, migrated to New York, North Carolina, and other territories where they felt they would be safer. Others joined the crews of the proliferating rebel privateers and many never returned. Still others became members of the Colonial Army and fought for the cause ashore. But the majority of Nantucketers chose to remain, not only because they hadn't the means to go but also because they were reluctant to leave their island home and their properties. Tied in with these motivations, undoubtedly, was the Nantucketers' inherent inclination toward pacifism and the substantial influence Quakerism had over the community.

Some historians and authors have labeled Nantucket as being neutral during the Revolution. In a sense, the islanders were. But it seems this situation can be looked at in another light too. The very fact that Nantucketers were willing to stick out the war at home, and defend their island if necessary, could be considered an act of patriotism in itself. In doing so, the Nantucketer faced a much worse situation than his civilian counterparts on the mainland, for Nantucket, being an island, was geographically "neutralized." The only contact and supply line was by boat. But the growing numbers of British warships and their privateers in the Sound were ready to pounce on and seize any island vessel which dared venture to the mainland. For the same reason, whaling, the only means of making a living, became impossible.

History tells us that at least some Nantucketers became active patriots. We have already mentioned those who joined the army and Colonial privateers. Perhaps the most well known fact is that many Nantucketers sailed with the famous John Paul Jones aboard his frigate *Bonhomme Richard* and displayed such excellent seamanship that the admiral said of them, ". . . the best crew I have ever seen and, I believe, the best afloat." It is in the records too that during the much-described battle between the British *Drake* and the Colonist *Ranger* under the command of Jones,

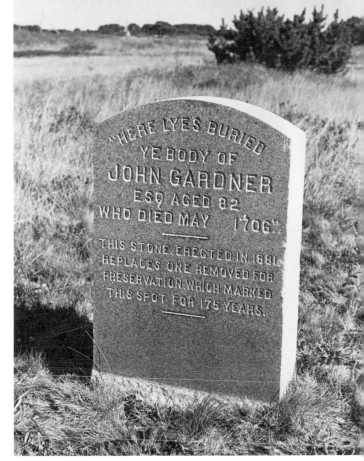

The grave of one of Nantucket's earliest settlers. Twenty yards from this spot stood the old meetinghouse of Sherburne.

"HERE LYES BURIED
YE BODY OF
JOHN GARDNER
ESQ AGED 82
WHO DIED MAY   1706"
THIS STONE, ERECTED IN 1881,
REPLACES ONE REMOVED FOR
PRESERVATION, WHICH MARKED
THIS SPOT FOR 175 YEARS.

twenty-two of the latter's crew of 134 were Nantucketers.

For those who stayed home, however, living conditions, especially in the last years of the Revolution, were deplorable. In the beginning, during 1775, the islanders turned their attention to farming and fishing for subsistence. They used local wood and, when that ran out, they were forced to use peat, which could be found in the many marshes and wetlands throughout the island. But gradually, as the war continued, these basic commodities became scarcer and were hardly enough to support the community. Some heroic attempts were made to get additional supplies. Earlier in the war, a few bold shipowners and their captains fitted out their idle whaling vessels and tried to run through the

45

enemy blockade and reach the West Indies. Some did make it and returned with precious supplies and marginal profits. Most didn't have such luck, unfortunately.

And there were individuals who, in small open boats, tried to sail to Connecticut and bring back wood and food to the island. Trips in these fragile craft were made at night during the stormiest weather to avoid detection. It was obvious that these daring Nantucketers preferred to drown than to be taken into the hands of the British off the Rhode Island coast. But sometimes they were spotted. "When pursued by an enemy," wrote Obed Macy, "they were sometimes subjected to so heavy a press of sail, as to run under and never rise again." Incidents such as these underscore the desperation of the islanders caused by their great suffering and need of provisions.

Throughout the war, the island was never really sacked by the British nor did the dreaded prison ships of the British ever come. But of Nantucket's original population of 4,500 just prior to the Revolution, 1,600 lost their lives. As for its once-proud whaling

Mooers Avenue, named after the bold Nantucket shipmaster who sailed his whaler up the Thames River in London only months after the end of the Revolution.

fleet, fifteen vessels were lost at sea and 134 were either captured by the British or sunk.

But the war failed to suppress the Nantucketer's spirit or his desire to continue whaling. This was dramatized by the fact that, only months after the ratification of peace with the British had taken place, the whaler *Bedford* under the command of Captain William Mooers, much to the utter dismay of the English, had the audacity to sail up the Thames to London. A newspaper of that city reported tersely, "she was loaded with 487 butts of whale oil, manned wholly by American seamen, wears the rebel colors and belongs to the island of Nantucket in Massachusetts.

"This is the first vessel which has displayed the thirteen rebellious stripes of America in any British port."

It is no wonder that two of Nantucket's present streets are named after this bold captain. Mooers Avenue is located on the outskirts of town near the cliffs which overlook Nantucket Sound. Mooers Lane is a quiet, shady street which runs off Fair Street nearer the center of town.

With the war ended, Nantucketers began to pick up the pieces and attempt to continue where they had left off in 1775. But rebuilding was no easy matter. The people were poor and their houses, which had been without paint or repair for seven years, made the town look bedraggled. Worse, the few vessels which managed to survive the war were in serious need of repair. But, among all this, there was a brighter side. Since there had been no whaling conducted during the war, many pods of right whales had reappeared locally around Nantucket's shores and, with the few vessels available, the industry was continued and gradually gained momentum over the next decade. By 1790, the population had recuperated and increased to 4,620 and the island fleet was steadily growing once more. (All vessels purchased by

A replica of the Beaver, built only recently, ties up alongside one of Nantucket's piers.

Nantucketers were built by shipyards on the mainland until 1810 when the island constructed her first shipyard adjacent to Brant Point, building and launching the ship *Rose*.)

It was the next year, however, when an event occurred which many believe was the beginning of Nantucket's "Golden Age of Whaling." This event was a voyage made by the ship *Beaver* under the command of Captain Paul Worth. The *Beaver* was the first Nantucket whaler ever to venture around Cape Horn, hunt sperm whales in the Pacific, and return to Nantucket. The *Beaver* proved that such a long voyage was both possible and profitable. The success of this voyage represented a great step forward in the progress of the island's whaling industry. From 1791 on, increasing numbers of Nantucket ships rounded the Horn and sailed into the Pacific in search of the sperm whale, sometimes being away from their island home for as long as three or four years.

But the *Beaver* was the first, and Captain Worth's description of the voyage is well worth quoting: "Captain Paul Worth, in a new ship of 240 tons burthen, called the Beaver, sailed from Nantucket on a whaling voyage, in the Pacific ocean, in the year 1791.

"The whole cost of said ship, fitted for the voyage, together with cargo, amounted to $10,212.

"She carried 17 men, and manned 3 boats of 5 men each, which left 2 men, called ship-keepers, on board the ship, when the boats were out in pursuit of whales.

"The principal part of her cargo, when fitted for sea, consisted of 400 bbls. iron hooped casks (the remainder, about 1,400 bbls. were wooden hooped,) 40 bbls. salt provison, 3½ tons of bread, 30 bushels of beans and peas, 1,000 lbs. rice, 40 gallons molasses, 24 bbls. flour.

"All the additional provisions during the voyage were 200 lbs. of bread.

49

"The ship was out for 17 months, and was the first belonging to the island, that returned from the Pacific Ocean.

"Her returned cargo was 650 bbls. sperm oil, worth 30 pounds per ton, 370 bbls. head matter, worth 60 pounds per ton, and 250 bbls. whale oil, worth 15 pounds per ton.

"The ship was not coppered. There were four other ships, belonging to Nantucket, whaling on the same coast that season."

Captain Worth's description omitted one very significant thing —the amount of courage it must have taken for him and his crew even to consider such a voyage. Not much was known about Cape Horn in those days. But enough was known to realize it was one of the most treacherous areas of water in the world. Almost every day of the year gale winds from the west, sometimes of hurricane force, forty- to fifty-foot seas, and unpredictable currents characterized the Horn. In later years, even the clipper ships with their fine bows and modified sails sometimes could not beat against the wind to round it and were forced to go before the gales, sailing across the South Atlantic, then past the tip of South Africa, "running their easting down" across the Indian Ocean, and finally to their destinations in the Orient and Pacific.

We must consider one additional point. If there was ever a vessel more poorly designed to round Cape Horn, it was the whaling ship. Her bluff bows were practically at right angles to the course she assumed, pushing the water out of her way like a tractor plows snow. Her sails were deep and awkward to handle, being single topsails and topgallant sails above, and, in ballast, she sat high out of the water. All these factors made the whaler about the worst vessel imaginable to go to windward. (One only needs to see the *Charles W. Morgan* at Mystic Seaport in Connecticut or the numerous models of whaling ships at the Nantucket Whaling Museum to understand what is meant.) Yet the *Beaver* doubled the Horn and so did hundreds of Nantucket and

The whaling ship Charles W. Morgan *in port (right) in company with the whaler* Wanderer *at Mystic, Connecticut. Note the whaleboats hanging from davits.*

New Bedford whaleships in the decades that followed. This says much about the seamanship and determination of these captains and their crews.

So the voyage of the *Beaver* opened up a vast new hunting ground for the sperm whale and, from 1791 until the War of 1812, Nantucket in general enjoyed the same kind of prosperity she had prior to the Revolution. Obed Macy describes the atmosphere of the island during this period: "The different branches of business to whaling were now carried on briskly; there was employment for all who were disposed to labor, the vessels arrived with generally good voyages, the markets were tolerably good for the sale

51

of oil and candles, a cheerful smile was seen on every countenance. This might justly be termed the golden age of Nantucket. It was a season of prosperity which ought to be remembered with gratitude to the Giver of all good."

Macy makes reference to candles. Candlemaking became a very lucrative offshoot industry of whaling. Candles were made from the sperm whale's spermaceti, a waxlike substance taken from the oil in its head. The first candle factory was built in 1772. At the peak of the whaling era in the 1820s and '30s, there were as many as thirty-five of these factories in operation, one of which is the present Whaling Museum on Broad Street near the Steamboat Wharf.

In 1795, the town's name was officially changed from Sherburne to Nantucket and the settlement continued to grow. By 1797, the town leaders decided to name the streets. In 1800, the population had grown to 5,617, and the Academy Hill school building was constructed on Academy Hill. Today it still functions as a grade school for children.

Perhaps the most loved and certainly the best-known structure which graces today's town outline and which has become synonymous with the image of Nantucket town is the old, golden-domed Unitarian Church building on Orange Street, just off lower Main Street. It was constructed in 1809. One year later, a melodious Portuguese church bell was cast in Lisbon, was bought by the town a few years later for five hundred dollars, and finally installed in the belfry in 1815. To this day, this very same bell tolls the hours night and day.

Most importantly, Nantucket's whaling fleet continued to grow, and a reporter, who visited the island in 1812, counted 116 vessels

The Unitarian Church and town clock whose belfry houses the Portuguese bell that has tolled the hours ever since 1815.

of all kinds. Of course many additional ships were at sea at the time.

Yet for a second period, Nantucket and her people were about to suffer the privations of another war. For three years, the War of 1812 raged. Although the islanders were less affected by this conflict than by the Revolution, they still experienced hardships and at the war's end in 1815, only twenty-three vessels were left. But as difficult as things were, Nantucketers dug themselves out as they had done before and rebuilt their whaling industry.

Little did they know then that in the next quarter century, the island would attain a prosperity they never dreamed of and become the third wealthiest municipality in the Commonwealth of Massachusetts, preceded only by Boston and Salem. In this future period, their whaleships would cover practically every ocean and sea of the globe, and the Nantucketer would draw praise from such giants as the author Herman Melville who wrote of him, "For the sea is his. He owns it, as emperors own their empires."

4

The Golden Age

FROM 1815 on, Nantucket's whaling industry moved forward to such an extent that, at the peak of this era in the 1830s, the island was considered the indisputable "whaling capital of the world." To give one an idea of just how enormous a production whaling became, one need only know that between the years of 1815 and 1860, Nantucket vessels brought home or sold elsewhere 1,313,946 barrels of oil. This staggering total can be perhaps better imagined when one realizes that one barrel contained approximately 31½ gallons. The greatest years of this production—in fact, the very peak of the whaling industry—occurred between 1820 and 1830 when 237 ships were in service, bringing in a sum total of 349,789 barrels of sperm oil and 36,105 barrels of whale oil. (Whale oil, as opposed to sperm oil, was merely oil from different species of whales other than the sperm whale.)

In this period of prosperity, most of the whale hunting was done in the Pacific where it was found that the sperm whale was

A whaling ship putting one of her boats in the water

most abundant. Therefore, voyages often lasted two to four years and whalemen, during their lifetimes, spent very little time at home with their families. A typical statement of that time comes from Captain George W. Gardner, who wrote, "I began to follow the sea at 13 years of age, and continued in that service for 37 years. I was shipmaster for 21 years. I performed 3 voyages to the coast of Brazil, 12 to the Pacific Ocean, 3 to Europe and 3 to the West Indies. During 37 years I was home but 4 years and 8 months. There were 23,000 barrels of oil obtained by vessels which I sailed in. During my following of the sea, from the best estimate I can make, I have travelled more than 1,000,000 miles."

The average size of a typical whaler was around 300 tons gross, 130 feet long, with a 30-foot beam and a 15-foot draft. Her try-works were located amidships and rarely did she have less than six whaleboats aboard. Her masts and yards were shorter than the conventional sailing ships, so that while her boats were lowered and chasing whales, a minimum crew could handle the ship. This skeleton crew usually consisted of the cooper, the cook, and the cabin boy.

During the entire life of Nantucket's whaling industry, 99 percent of the whaling ships were built on the mainland at places such as Haddum, Connecticut, on the Connecticut River and Mattapoisett, Massachusetts. This was more practical for ship-owners, rather than having to have all the building materials shipped to the island. From its conception in 1810, Nantucket's shipyard constructed only a little more than half a dozen vessels of substantial size.

At these mainland shipyards, the best possible materials were used in building a whaler. Live oak and yellow pine were imported from the South. The price of such a ship, prior to fitting out for a voyage, ranged around $22,000. When the vessel was completely constructed and launched, she was brought to Nantucket for preparation. Fitting her out for a trip to the Pacific would cost her owner, or owners, $18,000 more. Fitting out included everything from provisions consisting of beef, pork, and molasses to spare line and sails, around 4,000 new barrels, and even a supply of ink and paper for navigational purposes and the ship's log. All these things were brought out from the harbor in small lighters while the whaler was anchored off the Bar.

The Bar is a long, continuous shoal which runs 300 yards off Nantucket's north shore from the island's western extremity at Madaket toward its eastern end at Great Point. Earlier in the 1700s, whaling ships were smaller and had little difficulty getting over the Bar at high tide and sailing right up to the town piers. But as ships were built larger to accommodate the longer voyages to the Pacific, they were forced to anchor off the Bar to be unloaded and reloaded for outfitting. This Bar can be clearly seen today, especially at low tide with a brisk northerly wind, which creates a distinct white line of surf offshore. Of course the channel entrance to the harbor has long since been dredged, allowing a continuous flow of pleasure craft and passenger vessels to cross in and out of the Bar entrance as they please during the summer season. But in those days the larger whaleships were forced to anchor outside and north of the Bar. When one was finally fitted out, the crew would be last to arrive, numbering anywhere between twenty and thirty men.

To get to the Pacific, shipmasters had the choice of taking two different routes. The first was to sail south, passing Bermuda, to the West Indies, down along the east coast of South America and finally around Cape Horn to the Pacific. The second choice was to head east southeast across the Atlantic to the Azores and then continue south to close the southern coast of South America and the Horn. Both routes enabled whalers to stop at the West Indies and the Azores respectively for additional provisions. But, al-

The whaling bark Charles W. Morgan *under sail during the last years of her whaling career.*

though longer, the Azores route was more popular because it gave the ships a better slant to utilize the northeast trade winds and then, after crossing the equator and the doldrums (an area of calms on each side of the equator), the southeast trade winds.

Up to the Horn, at least, all sailing was generally peaceful and comfortable and the continual good weather enabled the crew to complete the fitting-out operations that were very often not finished when the ship weighed anchor from Nantucket. In the gentle tradewind belts, the cooper had time to build more casks, the sailmaker had opportunity to repair old sails, and the carpenter had a chance to repair and strengthen the whaleboats.

59

But the Horn was something else and the ship was battened down as tightly as possible. Relentless and bleak, this Godforsaken area, located almost exactly at 56 degrees south latitude, has put fear into the heart of every sailor who has seen it. Howling west winds, adverse currents, and mountainous seas forced the whaling ship to take a long tack southwards, sometimes as far as 59 degrees south where icebergs lurked and unbelievable cold froze men and rigging. Then, if the head winds backed slightly to the south of west, the ship would be put about on the port tack in the attempt to clear the Horn. Sometimes this took several tries, for often after the wind had backed favorably, it would veer again to the north of west and the ship would maddeningly find herself blown back to where she was a week ago. Because of these conditions, some captains ignored the Horn entirely on outbound trips, preferring to round South Africa's Cape of Good Hope and "run their easting down" across the southern Indian Ocean and on into the Pacific. Whichever way she went, the whaler ran into some whales along the way, but most sperm whales seemed to migrate to the southern latitudes of the Pacific.

When a pod of whales was seen, there was the familiar cry of "thar she blows!" from one of the lookouts aloft, and there were some shipmasters who offered small financial rewards for the first sailor to spot the mammals. The boats were then quickly lowered, manned by six men each and skippered by the captain and the officers. The ship, as noted earlier, was left in the hands of the cooper, the cook, and the cabin boy. Each whaleboat had at least 300 fathoms (1,800 feet) of line, at the end of which the harpoon was made fast. Once alongside a whale, the harpooner, using all the strength he had, hurled the weapon at the whale's head. Then, if he had time and the boat was in the proper position, he would use a special lance in the attempt to kill the whale. But often, in the melee, there just wasn't enough time to use the lance,

A whaleboat knocked skyward

and the infuriating creature would sound. In such cases, with the harpoon securely lodged in the whale's head—or "struck," in whalemen's language—the line was paid out. Sometimes whaleboats were towed along by these great mammals at terrific speeds, an occurrence which was aptly called "a Nantucket sleighride." Many times, to the whaleman's misfortune, instead of sounding a sperm whale would turn his wrath on the boat, smashing it to pieces with a flip of his huge flukes or actually biting a chunk out of it. All this ought to dispell any thought the reader might have about a whaling voyage being in any way romantic.

Once a whale was killed, it was brought alongside the mother whaling ship, made fast, and the operation of processing the oil begun. The average size of a sperm whale was 60 feet long. But if the creature was smaller than that, then, by block and tackle, it was made fast to the mainmast head and hauled aloft by its tail

Cutting up a whale

until it was almost out of the water. Afterward, the blubber was stripped, boiled in the tryworks, the resulting oil finally being poured into the casks and stowed in the hold. More often than not, the whales were too large to heave aloft and the blubber would have to be stripped while the whale was alongside and still in the water, making the operation more difficult. The normal male sperm whale yielded between 60 to 100 barrels of oil. By an unwritten law of the sea, the lower jaw and teeth were given to the crew. During lulls in the trip, the sailors made intricate sketches on these teeth, an art which came to be known as "scrimshaw." Through the years, this art has been handed down from one generation to another and today there are Nantucketers who still practice it, selling their valuable scrimshaw works in many of the gift shops around the waterfront. Although rare, whale teeth can still be found in certain foreign markets and, if they are not available, elephant ivory is used.

After a year or three years, depending on her luck, the whaler's hold would be filled with loaded casks of whale oil and she could return home. Some bore away directly to the east, sailing around the Horn and home to Nantucket. Others made detour stops before going home, to take on extra provisions and give their crews a long-needed change of scene. One of the most interesting of these detour stops was the Galápagos Islands which lay some 600 miles west of the Ecuadorian coast and where later Darwin was to find much material to support his theories of evolution as set forth in his *Origin of Species*. These islands became very popular among whalemen. Outbound whaling ships, which had been searching for sperm whales off the South American coast and working their way northwards before making their long runs into the Pacific, customarily stopped at the Galápagos, as did those ships going home. One of the main reasons ships stopped here, whether outgoing or incoming, was the fact that these islands teemed with wildlife. And in those days, there were few things more revered by sailors than fresh food. Besides having herds of wild goat and boar, as well as coastal fish, this archipelago was known for its giant land tortoises, some weighing more than 400 pounds. There were many of them, they made fine eating, and could be kept alive indefinitely with little food or water. Many a whaling ship weighed anchor from these islands with dozens of these giant turtles turned helplessly on their backs on the foredeck.

After a three- or four-year voyage, one can imagine the excitement which must have been generated when a returning whaler was sighted making for Nantucket's Bar. Wives who had probably first seen and identified their husband's ship from the "widow's walk" on top of their homes, swept up the children and

rushed to the piers. (Many of these original widow's walks still grace the rooftops of the town's countless old houses. In the beginning, these bannistered platforms were primarily constructed for the purpose of cleaning chimneys or putting out a conflagration—an ever-present fear with wooden houses—by dumping a bucketful of sand or water down the opening. Later, the walks proved to be natural observation posts for waiting wives.) As the captain and crew came ashore in boats, there must have been emotional reunions close to pandemonium as fathers hugged sons and daughters they had never seen before and husbands embraced their wives for the first time in years. And the women, certainly in tears, must have thanked God that their husbands were safe and home again, even if their menfolk were only to remain for a month or two before shipping out another time.

It has been my good luck to have been given permission to quote from the original logbook of a voyage made by the whaler *Mary Mitchell* from 1835 through 1838. The logbook is in excellent condition and beautifully bound. Its entries were made by the ship's officers in ink, faded brown with age, and display the meticulous penmanship of our ancestors. You can see similar logs of other whaling ships in the Whaling Museum and the Peter Foulger Museum. (This museum is named after the original miller, Peter Folger, who sometimes spelled his name with a "u," that being the old English way of spelling the word.) But for good reason, most of the logs are encased in glass, or kept in the vaults of the Atheneum, Nantucket's library. Insofar as I know, the log of the *Mary Mitchell* has never been published before.

Earlier we learned that the shipmasters had the choice of two routes to take to the Horn, and that some captains chose to bypass the Horn entirely and sail to the Pacific via the Cape of Good Hope and the Indian Ocean. It was this third route which the *Mary Mitchell* took, under the command of Captain Samuel Joy.

On the second day of the voyage out of Nantucket, July 15, 1835, this entry was made by Joseph McCleave, Jr., First Mate: "Ship Mary Mitchell from Nantucket towards East Cape [Azores]. Latter part tolerable clear, saw a ship or Brig to the West, the Brig enquired the longitude, let out the reefs & set the main & miz topgallantsails—employ'd fitting boats & other necessary jobs. Most of the Boys Sea sick."

On August 2, twenty-one days out of Nantucket, *Mary Mitchell*

Pursuing a whale

arrived at Flores, the westernmost island of the Azores, and hove to. This day's entry reads: "... Capt. went ashore with 2 boats ... the boats came aboard loaded with potatoes & onions. So ends laying off and on, 5 ships in Company." And, a few days later, "Remarks on board Tuesday, August 4th. Moderate breezes & pleasant, all hands employ'd pealing Onions to pickle, 4 sail in sight at sunset, set foretopmast Studensails."

When one reads this log, it is remarkable to note the large numbers of ships that seemed to be at sea during this period because, no matter where the *Mary Mitchell* was during these three years, First Mate McCleave frequently mentions the fact that other vessels were in sight. For instance, after departing Flores, she sailed south for the Cape of Good Hope. Two weeks out of Flores, when she was hundreds of miles at sea, McCleave wrote, "Remarks on board, Monday Aug 17th. Calm & baffling, with now & then a breeze from most all pts. 5 Barques & a schooner in sight, middle part light & baffling, latter part small

66

trades & fair, 4 sail in sight. All hands employ'd in Ship's duty, fitted a new larboard Boat & got her on the cranes at 11 AM."

More than two years later, *Mary Mitchell* nearly had a full cargo and was busy killing her last whales. McCleave's entry on Saturday, October 7, 1837, reads: "Strong Gales at SW headed to the SSE, middle part much the same, latter part moderate & pleasant, saw Whales, lower'd struck and killed 2, one of them sunk & the other turn'd up a long way to windward. So ends towing. Lat. obs. 33.30S, Long 185.20E."

This put the *Mary Mitchell's* position a few hundred miles north of New Zealand. On the following day, the logbook states, "Light breezes at SW & clear, at 2 PM finish'd got the whale alongside & commenced cutting, at 6 finish'd, lowered 2 or 3 times while cutting, but could not strike . . ." And once more on the next day, "Light breezes & clear, at 3 PM got 3 whales alongside, cut one of them in, got the larboard boat crack'd, Middle part employ'd Boiling, latter part light airs at SE & pleasant, all hands employ'd cutting. So ends. No obs."

After spending three years at sea, it must have been a momentous occasion when the last barrel of oil was lowered into the hold and the ship turned for home. Knowing human nature, one can conjure up in one's mind the hoopla and excitement of the crew at this point and imagine the captain calling all hands aft in order to make some sort of congratulatory speech. But the log of the *Mary Mitchell* records that Captain Samuel Joy sent his officers a letter!

Ship M. Mitchell at sea. Ltd. 34.30S Long. 174.00W
To the Officers of the ship—November 8th, 1837
Gentlemen, the avowed object of the Owners of this Ship in sending her on this voyage was to obtain a load of oil. You will therefore consult each other & give me your report in writing & signed by yourselves, whether that

purpose has been fulfilled & to what extent & you will oblige your's.

Respectfully, S. Joy

The officers' answer came promptly on the same day:

Nov. 8th, 1837

Ship M. Mitchell at sea
To the Capt. Sir,

We the undersigned Officers of said ship think that the purpose for which she was sent here for has been accomplished & that we have 40 or 50 bbls. of Oil more than we can get below deck & the sooner we can get in Port & fit for home the better for all concern'd.

J. McCleave	M. Swain
Marquis Shaw	John Hoeg
David O. Beard	Stephen Fisher

It seems the only logical reason for this peculiar procedure was to supply the owners with a record of the date and place when and where Captain Joy and his officers decided they had a full cargo and could go home. Whatever the reason might have been, there must have been some kind of celebrating aboard the *Mary Mitchell,* as well as on other whalers at such moments. It would be a good guess, indeed, regardless of the fact that it might not have been recorded in the ship's log, that Captain Joy most likely retired to his cabin, along with his officers, and broke out a bottle of rum. And most of the crew was probably doing the same thing forward in the foc'sle.

Be that as it may, the *Mary Mitchell* arrived in Woods Hole in May of 1838 where she discharged her cargo. On Sunday, May 27, First Mate McCleave wrote his last entry in the log: ". . . at 9 AM the Steamboat hook'd on & tow'd us to Nantucket. So ends this voyage. Turn'd out 2,568 bbls."

5

At the Home Port End

Wʜɪʟᴇ the whaling ships with their captains and crews were making their long, arduous voyages in search of the sperm whale, Nantucketers could be found in almost every part of the world. But things were happening at home too, and island life was bustling.

The community itself must have taken on the atmosphere of a boom town. On the waterfront and along lower Main Street and its tributaries, the offshoot businesses of whaling thrived. Constant activity was everywhere as ropewalks, cooperages, warehouses, and blacksmith shops engaged in their works and the candle factories produced candles to be sold all over the world. As far back as 1810, a shipyard had been established at Brant Point and now a few vessels were being built and sliding off the ways. Around or near the shipyard, sail lofts were busy cutting new jibs and topsails and, in other shops, carpenters used their adzes to shape out masts, yards, and booms. If one were to walk the cliffs which overlooked the Bar and Nantucket Sound to the north, one would have seen numbers of large whaling ships anchored, being fitted out for their next trips or, having just arrived, being unloaded by lighter boats which would bring the valuable casks of whale oil to the town in a steady stream.

The scenes at the Straight Wharf and other piers were busy ones too. Dozens of horse-drawn "drays" (two long planks on wheels harnessed to a horse) waited for the oil casks to be rolled up and secured before being hauled to the candle factories or warehouses for storage. And there would be other horses with their drays bringing empty new casks fresh from the cooperages to be loaded aboard outgoing lighters. One can even imagine a group of young boys watching all this bustle, dreaming of the day when they would strike their first whale and become bona fide harpooners.

As mentioned earlier, Quakerism had much influence on the life of the community. As a matter of fact, its ideology had an effect on almost everything. In his excellent book, *Nantucket, The Far-Away Island*, William Stevens writes concerning the dress of the period: "In 1803, for example, a young man in Nantucket was cast into outer darkness because he had tied his hair instead of letting it hang lank on his shoulders." Stevens writes that the Quakers even looked suspiciously at buttons, feeling that hooks and eyes were a great deal more proper. And all the women were required to wear bonnets and to act in a most humble manner.

Even architecture didn't escape Quaker influence. Those houses built in the 1700s, especially along Liberty, India, and Hussey streets in the town proper, were marked with lines of simplicity and modest design. Today you may walk up and down these streets and notice that most of the front steps lead up from the sides, rather than going up directly to the front doors, the Quakers feeling that this type of structure was less bold and more inconspicuous for an entrance.

A typical Quaker doorway of a house on India Street.

In addition, being a seaport of substantial significance and size, one wonders whether there were the usual bars, bawdy houses, and other establishments which have always catered to sailors arriving from extended voyages. If there were such places on Nantucket, they were very secret if, indeed, they existed at all. Again, this can be attributed to the Quaker religion and the great fear of any Nantucketer to do anything that could cast him out of the Society of Friends. But this influential hold that Quaker philosophy had on the community took a sharp decline in 1830 when a schism developed and a more liberal branch of the Friends, as they called themselves, was established. After this date, Quakerism lost its firm hold on community life and Nantucketers adopted more liberal habits of living.

Despite the thriving businesses of the candle factories, cooperages, ropewalks, and other activities which demanded the work of men, the great majority of the island's male population was at sea most of the time. The result was that the women often had to take care of their husbands' concerns on the island and manage the family businesses. It can be assumed then that the Nantucket woman of the 1830s was, by necessity, comparatively more independent than her counterparts on the mainland, having to make more decisions for herself.

Whether this situation directly or indirectly affected the character of Nantucket women is difficult to say. It certainly didn't do them any harm. Whatever, it is a fact that the island produced three quite famous women in our country's history. The first was Abiah Folger, daughter of Peter Folger who was mentioned earlier as being Nantucket's first miller in 1666. Abiah was the mother of Benjamin Franklin and today, about a half mile out of town on the Madaket Road, there stands a monument close to the road which marks the area where her original house was located.

Perhaps the most well-known Nantucket woman was Maria

The Maria Mitchell observatory on Vestal Street, near the house where she was born.

Mitchell, born in 1818. Like Abiah, she was a direct descendant of Peter Folger and, as a child, took a pronounced interest in mathematics and astronomy. She lived on Vestal Street, near the western fringe of town, where she had a small observatory built on the roof, from which she could study the stars with a small telescope which had been given her. When she was only twenty-nine, she made a discovery which would change her life. On an October evening in 1847, while observing the stars, she saw a new comet. Other astronomers were to see it days later, but Maria Mitchell was credited with its discovery and the King of Denmark, no less, awarded her a gold medal. After this, she was the first woman to become a Fellow of the Academy of Arts and Sciences. Later in her life, she served as head librarian for the Nantucket Atheneum and finally became Vassar College's first

73

professor of astronomy. Today, one can amble up quiet Vestal Street and, for a small admission, explore Maria Mitchell's house and observatory.

The third woman, Lucretia Mott, was born in 1793 in the house on Fair Street whose basement is now the restaurant, The Ship's Inn. Coincidentally, she was also a descendant of Peter Folger, as well as of Tristram Coffin, the original settler. Unlike Maria, Lucretia Mott spent very little of her life on the island. At a time when women didn't do such things, she was an excellent orator and she used this talent by voicing her antislavery beliefs and was also one of the earliest proponents of women's suffrage.

The town that raised these women was growing by leaps and bounds. The present Pacific National Bank building, at the head of lower Main Street, was built in 1818. In 1821, the town's first successful newspaper, the *Nantucket Inquirer*, was started and at present is still published weekly under the name of *The Inquirer and Mirror*. In 1827 two public schools were opened. At the same time, Admiral Isaac Coffin, who had been knighted by the King of England, visited the island. Although an admiral in the British Navy, he was also a direct descendant of Tristram Coffin, and the Nantucket Coffin blood running in his veins must have been the main motive for his visit. So delighted was he with the island and his relatives that he donated money which was used to construct the Coffin School off Upper Main Street. In 1837, the town ordered cobblestones from, reportedly, Gloucester, Massachusetts. They were carried over by schooner and put in place by the town on lower Main Street. In later years, Upper Main Street, as well as some of the side streets, would be cobblestoned too. Today the original stones still remain, a bit shinier and worn after more than a hundred years of use.

It seemed that progress and prosperity were everywhere. Of course, all of it stemmed from whaling. The ships brought home

74

The Pacific National Bank marks the uppermost limit of Main Street's business area and has been open for more than 150 years.

Worn by age and use, Nantucket's famous Main Street cobblestones have served the town since they were first laid in 1837.

the profits. And there were the men who owned them—the ship-owners and oil merchants. They, as much as the vessels and crews, were responsible in making the tiny island the "whaling capital of the world." These men reaped great benefits and they pumped energy into the island's economy.

Their elaborate legacies can be seen today. One only has to walk up the town's cobblestoned Main Street. At first, along lower

Main, one passes shops and stores. But when one reaches Upper Main Street and goes by the red-bricked Pacific Bank, the business section is left behind and one is confronted by the beautiful, elegant rows of mansions. Some are built of wood, others of brick; some boast proud, Southern-style columns guarding their front doors, while others have towering chimneys at all four corners that resemble sentinels. Some have the ordinary widow's walks on their rooftops and others cupolas. The scene is made lovelier by old, stately elm trees which were planted by the sons of one of the wealthy oil merchants: Zenas Coffin's two sons, Charles and Henry, in the 1850s.

It is difficult to say who was Nantucket's most famous and

One of the many mansions on Upper Main Street. This one was originally owned by Henry Coffin.

successful oil merchant and shipowner. They were all successful in their own ways. Some acquired their fortunes by going to sea as youngsters in their father's ships, sailing on several voyages. In time, they would buy a share in the ships as they were promoted through the ranks to finally become shipmasters. Eventually, either by inheritance or family transaction, they became full owners and began buying shares in other ships, building up a family fleet and even having their own fleet flags. As they grew older, they "swallowed their anchors" and stayed home to run the businesses.

There were other oil merchants who never went to sea. One of these was Joseph Starbuck, who was born in 1774 and was sixth in line to the original Edward Starbuck who spent that first winter in Madaket with his friend Thomas Macy in 1659. Although known to succeed in a variety of trades, including candlemaking, Joseph Starbuck was best known for his great fleet. As a shipowner, Joseph Starbuck operated twenty-three whaling vessels of varying sizes. His favorite six ships sailed a combined total of fifty voyages, bringing back over 80,000 barrels of oil worth approximately $2,500,000! Just before he died as an old man, his ship, the *Three Brothers*, after a four-year voyage, came back to Nantucket with the largest cargo of whale oil ever taken. In 1859, this ship unloaded 6,000 barrels, full to the brim.

During his career, Joseph Starbuck managed the profits and payments of his ships and crew, much like his fellow oil merchants He gave his captains $\frac{1}{16}$ share of the cargos, his mates $\frac{1}{21}$, his second mates $\frac{1}{37}$, the cabin boy $\frac{1}{120}$. These figures give a general idea how profits were shared among the crews. Joseph gave his shipmasters extra incentive by offering a $300 bonus if any one of them returned with more than 2,400 barrels.

Joseph Starbuck's legacy is very much in evidence today. In 1838, he constructed three identical, Georgian-type mansions

78

The "Three Bricks" on Upper Main Street, designed and built by Joseph Starbuck in 1838. He gave these houses to his three sons.

known as the "Three Bricks." After their completion, he gave one to each of his three sons, Matthew, William, and George. Today they still stand regally, owned by others and very much lived in.

Then there was Zenas Coffin, born in 1764. At an early age he went to sea and quickly became a shipmaster. Like Joseph Starbuck, he acquired a large fleet and, with it, wealth. When old Zenas died, he left behind him the great profits of whaling as well as real estate. The family business was then carried on by sons Henry and Charles, the elm tree planters, who, after the Civil War when whaling was dead in Nantucket, continued to manage the family business successfully by going into real estate. But Zenas Coffin, shipmaster, shipowner, and oil merchant, started it all. And the legacy he, his sons, and several of his relatives left behind is impressive indeed: *nine* Coffin mansions spread out on either side of Upper Main Street, extending from near the business section to just past the Soldiers' and Sailors' monument a quarter of a mile away.

Charles and Henry must have inherited their father's energies and foresight because, in the ensuing years, they did much for the community and Nantucket. One of their first ventures, as has been mentioned, was beautifying the town by planting trees. A lithograph made before 1846 shows lower Main Street with not one tree to be seen. This view of Nantucket's business section is strikingly bare and bleak. Charles and Henry thought so too, and in the spring of 1851, the two began planting elm saplings on each side of the street.

Surprisingly, they were met with a certain amount of criticism. A few people claimed that after the trees had grown enough, the high winds would make kindling out of their branches and break windows. Others argued that the trees in the future would render streets and lanes "as dark as a pocket." And still others grumbled

80

A few of the elm trees planted on lower Main Street by brothers Henry and Charles Coffin in 1852.

Sankaty Head lighthouse. Since 1853, her beam has warned mariners of the dangerous shoals off the east and southeast shores of the island.

that trees weren't meant to grow in sand. Just one look at the beauty of Main Street today would silence those dissenters.

But the town wasn't the only place the Coffin brothers were interested in beautifying. They were also anxious to develop forests. Between 1875 and 1877, using plants imported from England, Charles and Henry planted approximately 40,000 Scotch pine, fir, and larch trees around the east side of Miacomet Pond, an area about three miles southwest of town. Unknown to them at the time was the fact that several different varieties of heather seedlings had managed to cling onto the roots of these trees and were dislodged during the actual planting. Blown by the wind, these heather seedlings found suitable places to grow, and today one may find many patches of Scotch heather throughout the island. Of course, by then other Nantucketers, because of the Coffins, became interested in their own planting projects and some might have sent for, or brought back from England, heather seedlings and planted them in later years.

Such was Nantucket ashore during the height of the whaling days. But the island's whaling industry was bound to come to an end and there is an ironic twist in the island's history. In 1850, Sankaty Head lighthouse was built on the bluffs which Gosnold first saw in 1602. Its purpose was to guide the island's whaling ships around the southeast shoals and home to the Bar. But at the completion of its construction, Nantucket's supremacy as "whaling capital of the world" was being challenged by New Bedford and the island's own whaling industry was beginning to dwindle. Sankaty Head light was supposed to aid the industry. Since its construction it has guided many ships to safety, but its conception occurred when whaling had just about died out on the island. Therefore, it can also be considered a monument to that fact—a gravestone of a once-great industry.

 6

The End of an Era

A visitor in 1820 observed that Nantucket had fifteen to twenty operating candle factories and refineries, ten ropewalks, a bank, a museum, and an insurance office. In 1835, as the Coffins, Starbucks, Macys, and others had built and would build more mansions on Upper Main Street, Nantucket was considered the third wealthiest municipality in the Commonwealth, and her fleet provided much of the oil and materials for candles which literally gave light in homes throughout the world. But this monopoly the island held on the whaling industry was doomed for a number of reasons, and signs of its demise could be seen as early as in the late 1820s when, for the first time, New Bedford's fleet surpassed Nantucket's in tonnage. From then on, things went steadily downhill until, at the outbreak of the Civil War, the back of Nantucket's whaling industry was completely broken.

It is hard to believe that this was happening at all when one imagines the Coffins and Joseph Starbuck building their palatial homes, and when ships such as the *Three Brothers* as late as 1859 were coming home with 6,000 barrels of whale oil. But fate, discovery, and Nature herself played important roles in contributing to the death of Nantucket whaling. There were countless minor causes, but the major ones were:

1. The increasing build-up of the Bar
2. The Great Fire of 1846
3. The Gold Rush of 1849
4. The discovery of "earth oil"
5. The Civil War

THE BAR: This long sand shoal extending off the north shore of the island, running from the west end of Madaket almost clear to Great Point, caused no serious problems in earlier days. Christopher Hussey and others in the early 1700s owned small 40- to 50-ton sloops which could easily sail over the Bar at high tide, even when fully loaded. But at the turn of the century, larger vessels of

The shoal called the Bar can be seen here just below the horizon.

over 100 tons were being constructed as longer voyages were undertaken to the Pacific. The result was that when these ships returned fully loaded with oil, they couldn't get across the Bar, even at high tide, without going aground. So they were forced to anchor off it a few hundred yards to the north in the open roads. Lighters had to be employed to go to and fro from the ships to the wharves taking in the heavy casks of whale oil. After a few days, the ships were lightened enough to sail across the Bar, up the channel, and into the inner harbor to the town piers where the unloading of their cargos was completed. But the necessity of using the lighters at the start added much to the expenses of the shipowners and cut into their profits. That is why some oil merchants preferred to have their vessels unloaded alongside the docks at Woods Hole and the Vineyard. It saved them money and time, and afterward the ships could be sailed or towed home to Nantucket harbor, as we have seen, for instance, in the case of the *Mary Mitchell*.

At the same time, there were some foresighted Nantucketers who realized that the Bar would cause serious problems in the future. One of them was Zenas Coffin who, in 1803, led a group of islanders and appealed to the National Congress for funds to dredge the Bar at the channel entrance. Nothing came of this appeal. Zenas tried again in 1806. Again Congress did not act. But he was not one to give up easily and championed the issue constantly. In later years, Congress finally did come through with some appropriations. But all efforts to dredge an opening across the Bar and into the harbor channel were fruitless because as soon as the opening was dug, the tide and wind would simply fill it up with sand again, and the project had to be abandoned. What was really needed was a breakwater. The western jetty was built in 1881, after which dredging was successfully achieved. But this was much, much too late. The last whaling ship ever to set sail from Nantucket was the bark *Oak* on November 16, 1869.

For a period of seven years, between 1842 and 1849, one heroic attempt was made to conquer the Bar. A Nantucket man named Peter Ewer invented what was known as the "camel," a huge floating drydock that could lift fully loaded whaling ships high enough to clear the Bar. In tow and riding on this contraption, the whaler was ignominiously brought around Brant Point to the town piers. But building these camels, and the added overhead they caused the industry, made them impractical. Today one may see a large model of one of these camels in the Whaling Museum.

As said earlier, the Bar can still be seen today. Through the years storms have shifted the sands a little, but essentially it is on the same line. Once a problem, now it is hardly noticed, except by sport fishermen in their outboards who know that in late June and early July, the bluefish love to school up inside the Bar in a place that's locally known as the "Cord of the Bay."

THE GREAT FIRE OF 1846: Although there was a fire ten years before, which destroyed a hotel and a few shops, Nantucket has never known a conflagration as bad as the one which occurred on the evening of July 13, 1846. The fire started in William H. Geary's hat store on lower Main Street and quickly spread over the entire business district of the town, including some of the waterfront, wiping out 400 buildings and destroying $1,000,000 worth of property. The area of its devastation was immense. Starting at Geary's store (which was in the area of Buttner's at the corner of Union and Main streets today), it burned in a generally northerly direction, fanning out to the east and west as it went. Its perimeter was marked roughly by lower Main Street to the south, Centre Street to the west, Broad Street and halfway up North Water and North Beach streets to the north, and a good portion of the waterfront to the east.

To this day, there has never been a fire in town anything to the likes of the Great Fire of '46. Fortunately the mansions of Upper

The spot where William Geary's hat store once stood and where the Great Fire of 1846 started.

Right: The Atheneum, Nantucket's library. During the Great Fire, it was totally destroyed but rebuilt a few years later.

Main Street, the Pacific Bank, and all the houses south of Main and west of Centre Streets were spared. As a matter of fact, most of the residential areas in town remained unscathed, and the tourist is lucky still to be able to see hundreds of old homes, once owned by shipmasters and oil merchants alike, built so long ago. But the commercial part of town was for the most part leveled. All of the cooperages, many of the candle factories, blacksmith shops, ropewalks, sail lofts, and warehouses which stored countless barrels of whale oil went up in smoke and flames. All these businesses and stockpiles were an essential part of the whaling industry. Just overnight, thirty-six acres of these vital operations simply vanished. Thankfully, no one was killed, but one can eas-

88

ily understand how much the Great Fire crippled the island's industry.

Help came from the mainland. Under the command of Captain Borden, the steamer *Bradford Durfee* out of Fall River brought a few hundred people who aided and gave provisions to the destitute Nantucketers. During the immediate years, the islanders slowly dug themselves out and rebuilt the commercial part of town. But the damage had been done. In the year 1860, only six Nantucket whalers sailed from the Bar for oil.

THE GOLD RUSH OF 1849: As if the Great Fire hadn't done enough harm to Nantucket's whaling future, the Gold Rush of 1849 occurred, and there was as much excitement about this discovery on the island as anywhere else in the country. Crews deserted their whaling ships and joined up with merchant vessels bound for the West Coast. Even some shipowners sent their own whaling ships to California. Although "gold fever" hit just about everyone in Nantucket, the young were especially vulnerable. A young cooper, for instance, would quickly realize that on a hard-working and long three-year voyage, he would probably make less than $600. His share of $\frac{1}{60}$th of the cargo was indeed earned the hard way. But now all he had to do was to ship out to California where there was always the possibility that in *one day* he could make himself richer than all the Coffins and Starbucks put together! So there was a substantial exodus by Nantucketers from their own whalers, as well as by those who worked in the cooperages, ropewalks and other shops, the gold temptation being too strong. This only helped to deepen the crisis of the island's oil industry.

EARTH OIL: Three years later, in 1852, someone in Waltham, Massachusetts, discovered that "earth oil" could be refined into

90

kerosene. A few years after this, E. L. Drake began the modern petroleum industry by drilling and producing an oil well at Oil Creek, Pennsylvania, later to be called Titusville. This new oil burned better and was much cheaper than sperm oil, and its discovery was the crowning blow which, for all intents and purposes, killed Nantucket's industry and her candlemaking business. There was no longer a demand for Nantucket whale oil.

THE CIVIL WAR: The war only put the lid on the already empty bottle of Nantucket's whaling industry. Because of attacking enemy privateers and warships, the once-proud fleet, which had numbered in the hundreds, was slowly whittled away. All ship-building ceased and real estate on the island dropped to practically nothing in value. About the only good thing that happened to Nantucket during the war was that she sent 213 men into the Union Army, fifty-six more than her quota dictated. For this Nantucket was proclaimed "The Banner Town of the Commonwealth."

Figures show that the island whaling industry began its decline as early as the 1820s when New Bedford's fleet led Nantucket's. In 1846, New Bedford had sixty-nine registered ships to Nantucket's sixteen. And in 1857 new Bedford's fleet had grown to ninety-five vessels. In that same year, Nantucket could only boast four ships!

But history has forever decreed that the little island of Nantucket was the world's "Queen of Whaling" and that she led the way in that industry for well over a century. She had reigned supreme and her sailors had reaped the oceans' riches.

Before we leave the subject of whaling, it would be remiss to ignore the episode of the whaling ship *Essex*. There are two reasons for this. First, nowhere in the annals of maritime history can

91

there be found a more bizarre and unbelievable incident. Secondly, the story of the *Essex* and of her men underscores the strong character and courage of most Nantucket whalemen.

Built in Salem in 1796, the *Essex* was 238 tons. On August 12, 1819, she set sail from Nantucket with twenty men under the command of Captain George Pollard, assisted by his first mate, Owen Chase. On August 30, she stopped at Flores Island for fresh supplies and then headed for the Cape Verde Islands where she arrived sixteen days later. From there she took advantage of the trade winds and, just before Christmas, reached the latitude of Cape Horn. After five weeks, Captain Pollard was finally able to round the Horn and sail into the Pacific. He made several stops along the coast of Chile, and then cruised offshore the following summer and obtained approximately 800 barrels of oil. On October 2, the ship raised the Galápagos Islands where the crew replenished her fresh food supply with the well-known island tortoises. On October 23, the *Essex* left the Galápagos astern and headed due west in search of more whales.

The strange event occurred on November 20, a month after, and was recorded in detail in a rare diary written by First Mate Owen Chase, which now lies in the vaults of the Atheneum. It has been quoted often by other writers, including noted Nantucket historian Edouard Stackpole. One of the most recent books about the *Essex* incident is *The Wreck of the Whaleship Essex*, edited and compiled in 1965 by Iola Haverstick and Betty Shepherd, in which Chase's entire diary appears from beginning to end.

According to Chase's words, a pod of sperm whales was sighted on the morning of the 20th and Captain Pollard immediately had all four of the *Essex*'s boats lowered. While attempting to strike a whale, Owen Chase's boat was damaged and he had to return to the ship for repairs. While his boat crew was busy repairing the

92

Smashing of the ship Essex *by a whale*

boat, Chase noticed a large sperm whale more than 300 feet off the weather bow which was ". . . as well as I could judge about eighty-five feet in length." (To give one an idea of the relative size, the *Essex* herself was 101 feet long.) The whale lay quietly, spouting a few times, and then disappeared. Almost immediately it reappeared about 100 feet away and began making a run straight for the *Essex*. At first Chase and the others on board were not concerned, until it became obvious that the huge creature had no intention of changing its collision course. At that instant, Chase ordered the cabin boy to put the helm hard up in an attempt to avoid the whale. But it was too late.

The whale struck the ship with its head just forward of the

forechains, completely staving in the bow. "He gave us such an appalling and tremendous jar as nearly threw us all on our faces. The ship brought up suddenly and violently as if she had struck a rock and trembled a few seconds like a leaf." Those on board looked at one another in utter disbelief and were, as Chase describes, ". . . deprived almost of the power of speech." Then, minutes later, the whale returned again, and, at a greater speed than before, rammed the bow a second time before it finally disappeared.

With water gushing into the gaping holes forward, the *Essex* very quickly settled down at the bow. One can imagine Captain Pollard's reaction when he first noticed his ship. It was a calm day and there wasn't a reason in the world why his vessel, in just a matter of minutes, was sinking. It would be a good guess that when he first became aware of the disastrous state of his *Essex*, he thought he was seeing things. At any rate, all boats returned to the *Essex*, which had now turned over on her beam's end. After a quick explanation from Chase, Pollard ordered the masts cut, after which the ship righted herself somewhat and remained half afloat. For two days Pollard and his crew salvaged everything they could find in the way of water, bread, nautical instruments, tools, and miscellaneous provisions.

After two days of hanging around the wreck, Pollard came to a decision. There remained three boats containing twenty men, or an average of seven a boat. The nearest land was the Marquesas Islands 500 miles to the southwest and to leeward. But these islands had been known for their cannibals, and Pollard preferred to take on the sea as his adversary. He decided, therefore, to head southeast and try to make the 2,000-mile journey to the South American coast. So, at his order, the boats set sail, leaving the wreck that was once the *Essex*.

The occupants of each boat were immediately put on the

severest rations, just enough to keep them alive and to make their precious supply of bread and water last as long as possible. All three boats decided to stick together, not only for the feeling of security that comes from safety in numbers, but also to help any boat that might run into trouble. Captain Pollard was in command of the first boat, Owen Chase the second, and Second Mate Matthew Joy the third. Twenty-nine days later they raised Ducie Island, a small clump of land 2,500 miles west of the Chilean coast. After a month of a starvation diet, constant exposure, and never-ending bailing, the men were so weakened that it was all they could do to gather what food they could find on the island. Fortunately they found a source of fresh water to fill up their casks.

Despite the fact they had covered more than 1,000 miles since leaving the wreck, they were now an additional 500 miles away from the Chilean coast. Still, Captain Pollard was determined to sail east and make an attempt. After a week on Ducie, the ill-fated fleet prepared to set sail again. Three men, however, elected to remain on the island. In his diary, Chase wrote about his farewell to these men, believing he would never lay eyes on them again: "They seemed to be very much affected, and one of them shed tears."

Once more at sea, the three boats sailed in consort for the next two weeks. On January 10, the first man died. Second Mate Matthew Joy had been extremely weak for an extended time and his death was no surprise. He was given a proper sea burial. Two days later, Chase's boat got separated from the other two during a stormy night and he never saw the other boats again. Chase stubbornly continued to sail east. By the first week in February, one of his men had died and the others were so weak they couldn't lift their oars. All provisions had been consumed except for a pitifully small supply of bread and water.

Then, on February 8, Isaac Cole went mad and finally died in a fit. Chase kept Cole aboard during the night, intending to give him the usual sea burial in the morning. But when dawn came, Chase remembers, "Our provisions could not possibly last us beyond three days. Within this time it was not in any degree probable that we should find relief from our present sufferings, and, accordingly, hunger would at last drive us to the necessity of casting lots. It was without any objection agreed to, and we set to work as fast as we were able to prepare the body so as to prevent its spoiling."

On February 18, Chase and his two remaining seamen were rescued by the brig *Indian* out of London. Excluding his one-week stay at Ducie Island, Owen Chase and his two men had been at sea in an open boat for eighty-three days. Other sources tell us that shortly after, a few hundred miles to the south, Captain Pollard, who, like Chase, had nearly reached the South American coast, was rescued by the ship *Dauphin*. There was only one seaman left alive with him. Much later the three men who had chosen to stay on Ducie Island were picked up by another vessel. The third boat of the *Essex* was never seen again. Of the *Essex*'s original crew of twenty, only eight survived.

Being somewhat acquainted with the nature of the Nantucketer by now, it might not surprise the reader that all eight of these men who survived the awful ordeal went to sea again, some becoming shipmasters in the future. Only Captain Pollard himself had problems. After returning to Nantucket and spending time there, he was given another command. But the voyage was a dismal failure and after that, he was unable to find any shipowners who were interested in giving him a command of any of their ships. Being considered "jinxed," Captain Pollard was forced to retire ashore and "swallow his anchor."

The episode of the *Essex* shows in the most graphic way the character of the Nantucket whalemen. Of course there were exceptions, but for the most part it was men like this who made the glory of Nantucket whaling what it was. They, as much as the wealthy shipowners and oil merchants, were responsible for building the island's industry into an empire.

But in 1860 and after the Civil War, whaling was dead and seamen such as these, as well as their wealthy benefactors, would have to look in a different direction to maintain their livelihoods and keep the Nantucket community alive.

7

The Trend Toward Tourism

I~F~ one wanted to get away from it all where peace and solitude is only occasionally interrupted by the call of the herring gull or the sound of a lone vehicle once or twice every hour, he should visit Siasconset during the off-season months. Located eight miles southeast of Nantucket town, its original old fishing cottages and more modern summer homes, which are deserted in the winter, rest on a bluff overlooking the blue Atlantic Ocean. What makes Siasconset—or 'Sconset, as it's known locally—so quiet is not only the fact that it is isolated from town, nestled in one of the island's corners, but also the fact that only thirty-seven families live there all year round.

'Sconset, now and in the past, has always been the island's "other town," although it could hardly be called that. "Village" is a more appropriate description. At present it has a small post office, one general store, two gas pumps, a sandwich snack shop, and a church which caters to all religions. Except for the post

A quiet and narrow 'Sconset lane

office, all these establishments close down in the off-season months between October and June. But 'Sconset's seclusion during these months is very much a part of its charm. Around the original village most of the streets are one-way. There is a very logical reason for this. These streets, or more properly lanes, are so narrow that they can barely accommodate the width of a car. Old, shanty-like cottages with sagging roofs and crooked chimneys stand perilously close to the borders of these lanes, often only separated by a small picket fence. Sometimes, one thinks while driving around these tiny streets of 'Sconset that it is indeed fortunate that most of the front doors of these dwellings open toward the inside, safe from being sideswiped by passing cars.

In the summertime, the village's appearance changes. Roses grow profusely along fences and climb up the latticework of the houses. The "summer folk" arrive for their vacations and fill up their houses or rent available cottages. The population swells tenfold, kids dart around the shade-covered lanes on their bikes, and sun worshipers walk the 100 yards down the bluff, through Codfish Park and to the beach. The post office, general store, gas pumps, sandwich snack shop and church all open for business, as do two excellent restaurants and a tennis court. Yet despite this three-month period from June until Labor Day of abnormal activity, somehow 'Sconset manages to maintain a certain serenity. It also maintains an intangible feeling of aloofness from the world, even from Nantucket town itself, just eight miles away. Nothing underscores this aloofness and quiet isolation more than a simple sign one might notice as he walks down the bluff toward Codfish Park. Pointing in the general direction of the beach and the Atlantic Ocean beyond, it casually announces: 3000 MILES TO SPAIN. It simply makes one feel he has reached the end of the road—a beautiful end.

The history of 'Sconset dates as far back as 1676 when some of

100

'Sconset's famous sign pointing directly due east across the Atlantic Ocean . . . and across the water, 3,000 miles away, another sign points back at 'Sconset from the small village of Marbella, Spain.

the original settlers from Sherburne, the old town site around Maxcy's and Capaum ponds, started to build fishing "stages," or shanties. These dwellings were occupied by fishermen who, after their daily trips offshore in search of cod and bluefish, would use them as modest shelters. At about the same time, another village called Sesachacha, or Peedee Village, was built about two miles north of 'Sconset up the beach. Gradually during the next 140 years, however, Sesachacha Village "merged" with 'Sconset as the former settlement's houses were moved, one by one, to the south.

Originally, these fishermen's 'Sconset shanties consisted of just one room where all the cooking, eating, and sleeping was done. Although cramped, it was a lot easier spending the week fishing and living in such small shelters at nights rather than taking the long trek over the moors back to Sherburne each day.

In later years when the town moved to its present site, a trip to or from town could turn out to be a sort of miniature safari, especially after freezes or thaws. This was because the ruts made by the wagon wheels in the particular route that was current became so deep that the thoroughfare had to be abandoned and a new one created to traverse the moors. Today the road to 'Sconset from town is long, straight, and paved. Work was commenced on it in 1894 and the paving was completed in 1910. But before the paving, these wagon wheel ruts were still hazards during all the years since 'Sconset was founded. As a matter of fact, there are a number of Nantucket old-timers alive today who, as boys and girls, can remember those quagmired days.

There is one particular story these old-timers like to tell. It is a true story, although there is always a certain amount of embellishment in the telling of it. If the reader will study the map, he will see that the 'Sconset Road runs almost directly from town to the village. But just outside of town, there is another road that turns off the 'Sconset route and heads left for Quaise and other points more to the north. This is the Polpis Road (once referred to as Podpis) and it generally follows the south shore of the inner harbor before it winds gradually south and ultimately ends up in 'Sconset.

The old-timers will tell you that before the roads were paved, the ruts at the intersection where the Polpis Road bears away from the 'Sconset Road sometimes caused peculiar problems. As children, they recall that their parents frequently took them for Sunday rides in the family box-wagon. It was the usual custom to go to 'Sconset, but sometimes things didn't turn out that way. This was because, occasionally, the ruts at the Polpis Road intersection were so deep that a wagon could be involuntarily sidetracked and find itself and its occupants turning off onto the Polpis Road, as solidly entrenched in and at the mercy of the ruts' direction as a train on a track. Of course whenever this did happen, a place eventually could be found to get out of the ruts and the wagon could return to the intersection and continue on to 'Sconset. This is only to point out that at this intersection, as well as other spots on the island, the ruts sometimes caused novel interruptions.

Getting back to the beginnings of 'Sconset, the shanties were one-room affairs, but as Quakerism took hold in the 1700s, changes were made. One of the religion's facets was a passion for tidiness. Also the women got tired of being abandoned by their men folk for weeks at a time, and they began to move out to stay with their husbands. The combination of these two very influential elements led to substantial changes in the appearance of the typical 'Sconset shanty. First, they were generally cleaned up and then, as time went on, wings or ells were added to each end, becoming bedrooms or kitchens. Today many of these shanties remain virtually unchanged from their original state back in the 1700s.

'Sconset never really became an important fishing village like

A typical Siasconset shanty

some of the Cape Cod settlements. This was by no means caused by lack of fish. Had all the effort that had been put into whaling been instead redirected into the codfish industry, 'Sconset very likely would have been the codfish capital of the East Coast. But the fact was that Nantucket *was* so involved in whaling, at least until 1860. The only times when the village was seriously active in cod fishery was during the privations caused by the Revolution and the War of 1812 when Nantucketers were forced to fish lest they starve.

It was a mere twist of fate that 'Sconset and the fish never really got together. Even today the waters just off this quaint little village abound with cod and bluefish. Just a year ago, several Nantucket boats made trips off Sankaty and 'Sconset, returning with 800 pounds of cod each. And during the summer and fall, the rips off 'Sconset are considered by sportfishermen to be one of the prime bluefishing areas on the East Coast.

But although 'Sconset never became a significant fishing port, she played another role which was completely different and rather surprising, a role that helped Nantucket find that important direction to take to replace the vacant economic gap caused by the end of whaling. It was 'Sconset which started—at least in a local way at first—the original trends which ultimately led to tourism. It started after the Civil War when Nantucketers began the habit of taking their vacations in 'Sconset. Soon the village became the islanders' favorite summer resort. And should any visitors, friends or relatives, arrive on the island for the first time, it was certain their hosts would take them to 'Sconset on a sightseeing trip.

Then the islanders began buying the old cottages (if they didn't already own them), so that they could spend their summers in 'Sconset and then return to their regular homes in town during the winter months. As a matter of fact, there are several Nantucketers and year around residents who do this very thing today.

Things were happening in town too, all of which strengthened the island's trend toward the tourist industry. There were a few people already beginning to sell land, but the prime movers of the fledgling real estate business were brothers Charles and Henry Coffin, the tree planters. For the next twenty years after the war, these men and their sons made more than 400 land transactions. They were also instrumental in the planning and future development of Weeweeder on the south shore, then already called Surfside, where in later years a tourist "boom" would occur.

105

A view of the island's moors near Quaise

Others were opening up new hotels in town and home owners utilized their homes as boarding and guest houses. Land owners subdivided their properties into smaller lots and built cottages which they rented out to visitors. Now, instead of talking about whales and the Pacific, retired shipmasters sat on their porches and talked of how many "summer folk" were expected the coming year. By 1872, Nantucket had shifted all her energies from whaling to people, and had already become an established and popular summer resort.

All these efforts would have been fruitless, however, had there been no means by which to get the people to the island. Hence, the steamers played a most vital role.

The first steamer to come to Nantucket was the little 92-foot *Eagle* in 1818, eleven years after Fulton's successful experiment with steam. She sailed from New Bedford with sixty passengers and made regular trips to Nantucket until she was sold in 1821. In 1828, an even smaller steamer, the *Hamilton*, was put into service but lasted only one year. This was because she had so little power she could hardly stem the tide going up Nantucket's channel, let alone buck a brisk northerly wind on a return trip to the mainland. So she was only useful under the most favorable conditions. Finally, from 1829 to 1832, the *Marco Bozzaris* made trips to Nantucket and charged passengers two dollars.

These vessels during that period only made intermittent stops at the island, and it wasn't until 1832 that a reasonably steady service to and from Nantucket was inaugurated. The Nantucket Steamboat Company was formed and the steamer *Telegraph* was built, designed specifically for the Nantucket-mainland runs. She was 171 tons, 120 feet long, and burned wood for fuel. She was on the Nantucket route right up until around 1855. She was put on a tri-weekly schedule but, like her predecessors, served the island only during the spring, summer, and fall during her initial career. This was because her owners were afraid that the winter ice would damage her.

It is interesting to note that during the severest winters, when the conditions are right, not only the Nantucket and mainland harbors freeze over, but occasionally most of Nantucket Sound. This only happens when there is extreme cold and little or no wind for an extended period of time. Nantucketers call these "freeze-ups" and there have been many during the island's history. Just recently, no more than five years ago, there was a "freeze-up" which prevented the steamer from entering the harbor for an entire week. By the time the ice broke up and the steamer did manage to tie up to the Steamboat Wharf, the shelves at the supermarkets were half empty. The incident was duly reported in, no less, *The New York Times*. But "freeze-ups" have not occurred as frequently as in the last century, and the winter schedule of two steamers a day is seldom cancelled unless there is a particularly strong northeasterly gale. A footnote, too, about today's steamers compared to the earlier ones. Today, they are designed to carry the greatest amount of freight and cars. The old steamers, in comparison, were designed for the comfort of the passenger.

Getting back to the *Telegraph*, it was later discovered that, although not a powerful vessel, the unusual shape of her bow made her an excellent icebreaker. And so she was employed sometimes in the winter as well. This interesting characteristic of the *Telegraph* was described by Harry Turner, owner of the island's newspaper, *The Inquirer and Mirror*, in a book he wrote in 1910 entitled *The Story of the Island Steamers*. ". . . the peculiar model of the 'Telegraph' made her an excellent boat for battling the ice," Turner wrote, "and one old diary says that in 1840 she made a trip from New Bedford and found less than twenty miles

108

A recent "freeze-up" of Nantucket Sound and harbor. Because of the thick ice, the steamer was not able to enter the harbor for a whole week. Below: *The 1971 "freeze-up" stranded these commercial fishing boats.*

of clear water on the passage. Capt. Alden H. Adams, one of Nantucket's nonagenarians, informed the writer that at times, in order for the 'Telegraph' to make her way through the ice fields, the passengers would be requested to 'go aft,' so that the steamer's bow, which was of very peculiar shape and had a tendency to ride on top of the ice instead of through it, could be run well up on the floe. The passengers would then be called 'forward' and by their weight assist the steamer to break through the ice. This performance would be repeated many times . . . When the passengers would tire of the monotony which resulted from a long siege in the ice, they used to step out and walk alongside the steamer for some distance, in order to excercise their limbs."

The *Telegraph* must have done her share of towing as well. You will remember in an earlier chapter that the last entry in the logbook of the whaler *Mary Mitchell* states that the sailing vessel was taken in tow and returned to Nantucket. The tower had to be the *Telegraph*, for she was the only steamer servicing that area in 1838.

In 1842, the *Telegraph* was joined by the larger and more comfortable *Massachusetts*. The two stayed in service until 1855 when the *Island Home*, perhaps Nantucket's most popular and best-loved steamer, arrived on the scene. This latter vessel faithfully served Nantucket until close to the turn of the century. There were other steamers put into service during the last half of the 1800s, but they are too numerous to mention here. All were "side-wheelers" until just before 1900 when propeller-driven vessels were introduced.

The steamers helped Nantucket in a variety of ways. Before the Civil War they towed whalers across the Bar to the docks. They came to the islanders' assistance, as in the case of the *Bradford Durfee* after the Great Fire of '46. They brought provisions and mail, and they established in later years a constant and depend-

The Naushon *rounding Brant Point on her way back to the mainland. She is respresentative of the modern steamers used today.*

able link with the mainland. But by far the most important role they played for Nantucket was that of a steady conveyance to the island for the tourists. As the steamer service became more frequent, increasing numbers of tourists were able to come to the island. Word was spread around and Nantucket quickly became one of the most popular resorts in New England. Because of the steamers, the tourist industry grew to the point that, by the turn of the century, Nantucketers were depending on this new business as much as they had on sperm oil seventy years before.

111

 8

Of Trains and Autos

W<small>HEN</small> one lives on an island and is part of its community, strange happenings and incidents, most of little importance, seem to occur which one rarely sees in towns on the mainland. It is not my intention to explore the why of this phenomena. I only point it out as a statement of fact which can be underscored by one of the most commonly heard utterances on the island. "It could only happen on Nantucket" is heard time and time again throughout the year. A three-day winter nor'easter can easily prevent all boats and planes from coming to Nantucket, and soon word will rapidly spread that the bread shelf at the supermarket is nearly empty and only English muffins are left. Recently there was a rumor that a traffic light was going to be installed on the 'Sconset Road. Since there have never been any traffic lights on the island, someone was heard to say that, if he weren't such a law-abiding citizen, he would fetch his shotgun and "go out in the middle of the night and fill the darn thing with buckshot."

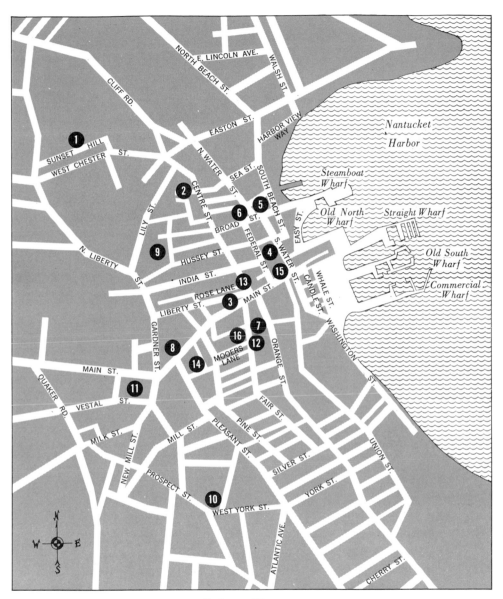

Points of Interest

1. Oldest House
2. Old North Church
3. Pacific National Bank
4. Atheneum
5. Whaling Museum
6. Information Bureau
7. Unitarian Church
8. The "Three Bricks"
9. Academy Hill school
10. Old Mill
11. Maria Mitchell home
    and observatory
12. Episcopal Church
13. Methodist Church
14. Baptist Church
15. St. Mary's Roman Catholic Church
16. Historical Association
    Quaker Meetinghouse

But there have been incidents in Nantucket history which have followed a much grander scale, and one of them was the fact that between 1881 and 1917, this little island had a railroad. We have learned that Nantucket was once the "whaling capital of the world" in the early 1820s. This fact is miraculous enough. But a railroad? One's first reaction to this might well be that it was satirical to have a railroad system on such a small island, as ridiculous as, say, building an eight-lane superhighway on Block Island or digging a subway system under the hills of Cuttyhunk. Yet when one realizes that Nantucket at this period was headed full tilt into the tourist trade, one might have second thoughts and admit that it might not have been such a crazy idea after all.

Long before the advent of the Nantucket railroad, Henry and Charles Coffin and their sons incorporated the Nantucket Surfside Land Company in 1873. Their capital was $200,000 and they began selling lots immediately. When the surveyors came to the island in 1879 to survey the likely routes for a possible railroad, one can imagine the delight of the Coffins and their willingness to cooperate with the railroad promoters. By this time Charles was in his eighties and had little interest. But his brother Henry and grandson Charles were very enthused about the project and obviously were influential in eventually having the route pass through Surfside. A 100-foot long depot was built there in 1880 which not only boasted a large pavilion but also a kitchen and restaurant.

After a number of ideas for different routes, the railroad promoters finally decided on one in May of 1880. All the equipment had arrived and work was begun, building a bed and laying the tracks. The ultimate plan was to link the town with 'Sconset, via Surfside and the south shore. Taking things by stages, the track was first laid directly to Surfside. Work on the extension to 'Sconset would come later.

114

Surfside on the south shore—a mile of the island's fifty-four miles of white beaches.

The route started at the Steamboat Wharf, curved in a southerly direction along what is now Easy Street, and hooked up with Candle and Washington streets. Then it continued straight, leaving Washington Street, passed the area where the Nantucket Shipyard now stands, afterwards curving more to the west, traversing Goose Pond by means of a causeway. Continuing in this general direction, the tracks crossed Orange Street near the present-day Hatch's Package Store, and on through a farm owned by a man named Hooper where Hooper Farm Road is now located. From there the tracks headed straight for Surfside through the pines and finally over the moors to the depot. The length of this route was a mere three miles and the rails were of the small-gauge variety, being three feet apart. Just a little earlier, in April, legislation had been passed and the Nantucket Railroad Company had become a reality.

Laying the tracks to Surfside was completed and, in late spring of 1881, the rolling stock arrived by barge. There was a locomotive named the *Dionis*, a coal tender, and two open coaches which could accommodate as many as eighty people each. The first run to the Surfside depot was made on July 4. The entire trip took only a few minutes and it was reported in *The Inquirer and Mirror* that all passengers enjoyed the ride to the fullest extent, the only complaint being heard from an individual who suggested the ride wasn't quite long enough. That first summer the little train netted $2,110 for the Nantucket Railroad Company, carrying 30,135 passengers.

For the first few years things went relatively well and the railroad seemed to have a solid future ahead of it. The following summer was a repeat of the first. People were shuttled back and forth between the town and Surfside, and picnics, clambakes, and dances became common occurrences. In 1883, Surfside suddenly not only had a 100-foot depot, but also a hotel. The Coffins and their Nantucket Surfside Land Company purchased a hotel in Rhode Island. Under the supervision of Henry's son, Charles, it was dismantled, shipped over by boat, and rebuilt near the depot. Appropriately, it was called the Surfside Hotel. Its construction marked the peak of what was known as the "Surfside Boom." By 1884, the tracks were extended all the way to 'Sconset, fringing the bluffs and hills overlooking the south shore, over Tom Nevers Head and down to Low Beach where the island's coast makes its turn toward the north and finally to 'Sconset.

But despite the excitement of the promoters over the acquisition of a new locomotive, the 'Sconset, this route along the south shore to the village was doomed from the beginning. Both winter and summer storms lashed at the south shore, eating away at the bluffs and threatening the railroad bed, even inundating it at times. On a number of occasions, parts of the tracks had to be moved farther inland and other sections were in constant need of repair. Finally the sea won out, burying the tracks to 'Sconset in sand, so that the train could go only to Surfside. By the turn of the century, new owners took over the railroad and an alternate route following the general direction of the 'Sconset Road and bypassing Surfside was built. The "Surfside Boom" ended and its depot and hotel were left to collapse from lack of repair, seas, and wind.

For seventeen more years, from 1900 to 1917, the little railroad operated nearly every summer. It was never a financial success. But undoubtedly the novelty of its very existence on the island induced many a tourist to come to Nantucket for the first time, returning to his mainland home not only extolling his adventures on the train, but, more significantly, the general charm and beauty of the island herself.

There are older people today who remember the train when they were young boys and girls. One of them is a sprite Nantucketer in his seventies who loves to talk of the old days. "Oh sure, I remember the train. Never did take a ride on it though. But I do remember us kids swimming in Goose Pond when it was hot. That old train used to go by and we all used to wave at the passengers, no matter whether we knew them or not. I remember too the little toot it made just before crossing Orange Street. You know, when they broke up the railroad in '17, some wise Nantucketer took a whole lot of the ties and sold them as fence posts."

Another Nantucket senior citizen who remembers the train says, "Yes, I did ride the train. Don't remember too much about it. But I do recall that it went quite fast and that most of us Nantucketers used it for fun more than anything else. And I remember its cute little whistle. All of us do, I think."

Sadly, the Nantucket Railroad went too much into the red in 1917. Operations were stopped and the track and rolling stock was sent to Europe to help the war effort. Today one is able to see clearly the causeway which crosses Goose Pond and the Creeks, still able to discern the railroad bed in places and, if one is lucky, find an old spike or two buried in the sand at Low Beach near 'Sconset where the tracks descended from Tom Nevers Head. Aside from this, the only tangible evidence that a railroad existed is, oddly, a restaurant. One of the coaches never left the island and was eventually moved to its present site on lower Main Street. It was then converted to a restaurant, first called the Pullman Car and then Allen's Diner. Later, under new management, a wing was added and now the coach has become the bar of the restaurant called The Club Car. The site of the coach couldn't be more appropriate. Not twenty-five feet beyond is the corner of Easy Street over which the old railroad tracks began their journey to Surfside and 'Sconset.

There were a number of reasons why the railroad was doomed.

118

The last remnant of the Nantucket Railroad—a coach which is now used as the bar for a popular restaurant on lower Main Street

Naturally, World War I dealt the fatal blow. But if it hadn't, and the train had managed to keep going, sooner or later the emergence of the automobile would have probably been its undoing.

The automobile has had quite a history since it was first introduced to Nantucket and, to this day, the relationship between it and the island has been a shaky one indeed. This relationship really started as a confrontation in 1913. A Nantucketer named Clinton B. Folger went to the mainland, purchased a five-passenger Overland, learned how to operate it, and earned his permit. Then he brought it back to the island. At first there were mixed reactions among the islanders. They were naturally curious about the invention, but at the same time wary of it. Some felt that the Overland's noise would frighten their horses and cause injury to both animal and rider. After deliberation, the town officials finally

119

Clinton Folger, his Overland, and his team of horses. (Courtesy of Mr. and Mrs. George Pinault.)

decided that Folger's new acquisition was not in the best interests of the island. Although Folger had been contracted by the United States Government to deliver mail with his Overland, he was summoned to court several times, the local judge fining him fifteen dollars for driving in the town. Later that year at the town meeting, the problem was put to a vote and the result was that all automobiles were banned on the island.

But Clinton B. Folger was not only a serious automobilist, he was also a Nantucketer with an unusual amount of inventiveness. Now that there was a law prohibiting him from using his Overland, he didn't dare drive it on the town streets anymore. However, he came up with a master plan. The Commonwealth of Massachusetts had not banned automobiles on the mainland. And the 'Sconset Road (or Milestone Road, as it's often called), all eight miles of it, was owned by the state! That meant he could drive on it, and all the selectmen and town officials put together wouldn't have the power to stop him. How to get the Overland from his house in town to the start of the 'Sconset Road? Easy. He

120

simply hitched his team of horses to a small wagon and towed the automobile out of town to where the 'Sconset Road began. Then he unhitched his horses and drove away to 'Sconset. During those war years, it became a familiar sight to see Clinton Folger hauling his Overland, which bore signs for U.S. MAIL on front and back, with his team of horses, past the post office and up Orange Street to the start of the 'Sconset Road. All during this period he was actually doing the town a favor by carrying mail as well as offering a unique taxi service.

But despite this, voting in the town meetings of 1915, '16, and '17 upheld the ban. More and more people, however, were beginning to realize the practical use of Clinton's "horseless carriage" and, in the meeting of 1918, the ban was lifted by the town voters. A week after the ban was lifted, a grand total of eleven cars was on the island.

One can imagine how Clinton Folger felt. He opened a repair shop on the corner of South Beach and Sea streets. For years this same building has been Cook's Cycle Shop, but on the old, graying shingles facing Sea Street, one can still make out the faded block letters, AUTO REPAIRING. Such is the legacy Clinton Folger has left us.

Today there is still talk about the presence of cars, and their relationship with the island is anything but solidified. For the past decade, the numbers of cars coming in the summer has literally reached the saturation point as the figures in the first chapter indicated. The Steamship Authority tells us that in recent years it brought nearly 10,000 cars to the island between June and September. Nantucket is a small island and most of the streets in town were never meant for automobiles in the first place, presenting a system of complicated, narrow, one-way streets and lanes which often confuse visitors during their vacations on the island. Every year the press comes out with editorials offering sugges-

121

Tourists debarking from one of the Hyannis ferries at the Straight Wharf.

tions about how to keep down the car population. But there doesn't seem to be any immediate answer. Many—summer residents and Nantucketers alike—wish that the island would be similar to Bermuda where only the "putt, putt" type of motor bikes are allowed. But in Nantucket's case, unless there was some unusual legislation pushed through, banning cars would be illegal. This is because whenever you pass through the State of Massachusetts and buy gasoline there, the tax you pay gives you the liberty to go anywhere you want to in the state. It's true that Nantucket is the only place in the United States that, in itself, is town, county, and island combined, but the island is still a part of Massachusetts. And so the talk just goes on, pro and con, as it had in 1913 during Clinton Folger's time.

Although the automobile has recently become a serious prob-

lem, there is no doubt that it has helped the island's tourist boom
immensely. From the turn of the century and after the auto ban
was lifted, a real tourist business began moving. More hotels were
built. Guest homes and boarding houses proliferated. Restaurants
made their appearances in and out of town. An airport was constructed. And so, during much if not all of this century, almost
the entire economy of Nantucket has been geared for tourism and
ways to attract visitors. And it is working. It wasn't so long ago—
perhaps ten or fifteen years or so—when seeing a tourist on a
warm February weekend was an exception. Now it has become
quite common to see tourists during any month of the off-season
if the weekend weather is nice.

From whales to people to make a livelihood is an odd transition
indeed. Tourism is, perhaps, less glamorous, yet one can only
think that it has its advantages over approaching a 60-foot sperm
whale in a small wooden boat with a crude harpoon.

*The Nantucket airport whose runways are long enough to accomodate
commercial jets.*

 *9*

Modern-day Nantucket

Today Nantucket is one of the most popular summer resorts on the East Coast. Islands have always seemed to lure people, and Nantucket offers much more than her beaches and cooling breezes. She has her history, which she has been able to preserve, a history which her people are very proud of. The old mansions of the Macys, Coffins, and Starbucks still stand in dignity on Upper Main Street, the town's main artery which remains cobblestoned. The Old Mill on Prospect Hill, built in 1746, continues to allow the wind to turn its old, creaking vanes and you can go inside and actually watch corn being ground as it was originally done. There are dozens of places in town that have, in fact, remained virtually the same since the eighteenth and early nineteenth centuries. If there has been any change at all, it is that the trees have grown

Nantucket's last remaining mill—the Old Mill. It still operates and grinds corn for tourists to see.

124

A quiet inner harbor, look-
ing north from Pocomo
Head with Coatue penin-
sula in the background.

taller and the forsythia and rose bushes have been planted more recently by new occupants. As we learned earlier, there are no traffic lights on the island, no billboards cluttering the country-side, and only one motel which, under the strict regulations of the Historic Commission, is in keeping with traditional Nantucket architecture and is shingled and attractive. And, for the same reason, the A&P is probably one of the more charming looking supermarkets in the country.

Since World War II, there have been clusters of developments built at Madaket at the west end, Hummock Pond on the south shore, at Pocomo Head, the large peninsula which juts out into the inner harbor, and at Tom Nevers Head near 'Sconset. And in the 'Sconset vicinity, there is one of the only loran stations on the

East Coast, a facility which aids ships and airplanes navigating the North Atlantic.

The perimeter of the town is slowly widening as new homes are built each year, but compared to most other New England towns, Nantucket has managed to escape, for the most part, the chain stores and restaurants, the gaudy neon signs, and the hot dog stands of progress. This is because long ago the islanders foresaw the dangers threatening Nantucket's preservation and realized that only through popular demand and legislation could they keep the island as nearly as possible the way she was hundreds of years ago. One can still drive six miles along the 'Sconset Road and see nothing on either side but trees, or venture along one of the many sand roads over the moors which lead to Saul's Hills, the heart of the island, without seeing a single dwelling. Without diligent efforts on the part of the town and various private sectors, Nantucket could have become like any other of the resort towns along the mainland coast. Hopefully, these efforts will continue to be successful in the future.

Understandably, Nantucketers have strong feelings about their island. Historian Obed Macy's comments about the inhabitants being "attached to their place of nativity" might well apply today as well as in 1760. Nantucketers are proud of their origin and will be quick to tell you about it. Much weight is given to the fact that one was born on the island. If one is so fortunate, he or she is considered a true Nantucketer, and that is simply the only way one earns the right to be called such. If someone was born off-island, came to Nantucket as a baby, and lived there until death, this still wouldn't count. The island may have been home for two years or twenty, but that person will always be an "off-islander." Being known as a native Nantucketer is a hallowed honor. One island businessman owns a license plate with the spelled-out word NATIVE on it.

This Nantucketer's license plate clearly indicates the pride he has in his heritage.

More than a half million people visit the island every summer. Unlike the old days in the 1800s when steamer service was either nonexistent or intermittent at best, dozens of ferries carrying cars and people, and scores of planes shuttle back and forth from the island to the Cape, Boston, and New York. Generally this summer entourage can be categorized into four groups: (1) The day-trippers who arrive from Woods Hole or Hyannis by boat, take the island tours in taxi vans or buses, and return to the Cape in the evening; (2) the ten-day to three-week vacationers who rent cottages or houses with their families and usually return each summer; (3) the armada of visiting yachts which fill up the hundreds of piers on the waterfront and anchor in the harbor; (4) the summer residents who stay the entire season and who own their own land and houses.

Although, of course, there are exceptions, the summer resident generally is the most dependable returnee, has the most interest in the welfare and future of the island, and is most likely to become involved in Nantucket's community activities. This is natural, since, of all the groups, the summer resident is the only one who can afford the time. Indeed you will find many who haven't missed a summer in Nantucket for thirty or forty years, and a few will come back during Thanksgiving, even Christmas, to enjoy their holidays on the island.

There are many in the second group too, the ten-day to three-week vacationer, who love the island as much as the more fortunate summer resident, and who have contributed to it and made friends with the Nantucketers. The same can be said for the yachtsmen, although on a lesser scale, for they are understandably more occupied with their boats than anything else. As for the day-trippers, it is difficult to determine how many return after their initial visit. Probably a few are just transients, but it is likely that the majority do return, possibly to become members of the other groups, having become victims of Nantucket's charm.

When one adds up all these groups of "off-islanders" who arrive at different times between June and September, the figure of 500,000 is a conservative one. What is it that attracts so many people to Nantucket? Aside from her historical significance, Nantucket's charm lies in her unique scenic beauty and climate. The countryside is, if anything, more like England than mainland U.S.A. It is marked by gently rolling moors and broad vales of heathland. Among these hills heather grows and, especially around the town, the Scotch broom in May and June blossoms into flowers of such yellow brilliance that the beauty of the forsythia plants in April is forgotten. Then there are the dunes, one never quite like another, and fifty-four miles of white beaches which beckon to swimmers, sun worshipers, surfers, and fisher-

Visitors headed for guest houses or the buses and taxis at lower Main Street which offer daily tours.

Right: *Young's Bicycle Shop, one of the busiest and oldest on the island.*

.men alike. The prevailing southwest wind blowing off the Atlantic keeps the island's temperatures down to five or ten degrees lower than those of the mainland. (The opposite works in the wintertime, the water acting as a warming aid when the wind blows over it.) If one wishes to get out on the water, there are many sailboats and charter fishing boats available. Even when it rains, one can spend an entire day browsing through the Whaling Museum and the Peter Foulger Museum which are side by side not far from the Steamboat Wharf.

Nantucketers themselves look forward to the summer with mixed emotions. Generally, they are accustomed to the influx of tourists and the population exploding from 5,600 to possibly ten

130

times that in any given day, and they quietly adapt to the change. For the many who operate summer businesses—gift shops, restaurants, hotels, rooming houses, sportfishing boats for charter— the tourist trade in the summer will have to tide them over through the coming winter. These Nantucketers welcome all the income they can get, for winters are sometimes lean. One of the most popular bicycle shops in town rents a fleet of 800 bikes and there are several days during the summer when the shop is "rented out." There are at least a half dozen additional cycle shops, and it is obvious that this two-wheeled conveyance is the most popular and practical way to see Nantucket. One sees bicycles all over the island.

Restaurant owners capitalize on Nantucket's history by giving their eateries names like Cap'n Tobey's, The Ship's Inn, Moby Dick, and The Skipper. The hungry visitor can't fail to find at least one thing to remind him that Nantucket was once a whaling center. It could be a harpoon hanging on the wall (most likely just a copy today) or a painting of a sperm whale's huge flukes smashing a small boat to pieces. The Brotherhood, on Broad Street just a block from the Steamboat Wharf, has the decor and atmosphere of a typical nineteenth-century pub.

In recent years a financier named Walter Beinecke has completely renovated the waterfront piers, an area which was becoming rather dilapidated. Hundreds of new slips were built and electrical outlets and water installed to accommodate and attract yachtsmen. Lining the piers, he has also erected a host of small shops which he rents to assorted craftsmen and shopkeepers every summer. The architecture of the waterfront has kept to Nantucket tradition and even old-style street lamps light up the wharves at night.

Looking toward the Straight Wharf, financier Walter Beinecke's waterfront improvements are clearly evident.

Once the rush of summer is over—by Labor Day and 500,000 "off-islanders" later—most Nantucketers are relieved and ready to embrace the quiet that comes. Suddenly he or she gets the feeling that the island is his once more, that favorite parking place across from the post office is always vacant again, and going to the supermarket is more of a social event than an ordeal. The country roads are strangely empty of bicycle riders, and the footprints on the bathing beaches are replaced by only tracks of gulls.

Yet when winter comes, things don't come to a standstill, although the pace slows down considerably. Many places close down until the next season, but essential services keep operating, of course—the banks, insurance companies, the supermarkets, the two drug stores on Main Street. Add to this the gasoline stations, the liquor stores, construction and lumber companies, and general house maintenance crews, and one realizes that there are a substantial number of available jobs. House maintenance in particular is very active because hundreds of summer homes are left vacant and need care and repair. For recreation, a bowling alley operates daily, high school football games featuring the Nantucket Whalers become big affairs, local basketball teams form leagues, there is bingo on Friday nights, and there is even a paddle tennis court. Something seems to be going on all the time.

For quite a few Nantucketers, the winter brings out the ancestral salt in their veins and they find themselves inextricably linked to the sea. Outfitting small twenty-foot boats with outboards, they take advantage of the scallop season from November to March, fishing the inner harbor and the west end off Madaket and Tuckernuck Island. It isn't the easiest way to make a living. Hauling dredges during a raw, windy January day for eight hours isn't fun. But neither was whaling. Later in the winter, others venture off the backside of the island in larger boats and fish for cod off the bluffs of Quidnet and Sankaty Head where Gosnold

134

Byron Coffin, thirteenth generation of Tristram Coffin, unloads his scallop catch on a cold January day.

first saw the island in 1602. And just recently, several modern deep-sea lobster boats have been laying their pots well offshore to the southwest of the island.

Still others, mostly older, primarily wait for the coming of the warm weather again. Almost without exception, these Nantucketers at some point in their lives have been to sea. They might have owned their own boats and fished off the shores of the island for the sport of it. Or they might have spent time on a commercial dragger, or skippered a sportfishing boat, or acted as a paid captain of a yacht, or scalloped in their younger days. Often you can see these Nantucketers drive to the Jetties beach parking lot which overlooks the Bar and Nantucket Sound to the north. They stay for a while, turn off their motors, and stare out to sea. Perhaps they are thinking of family matters or about some choice bit of gossip going around town. But I would bet that many times they are dreaming about their days at sea, just as their ancestors must have done before them. It's just something that comes naturally for a Nantucketer. "The Little Grey Lady of the Sea" holds a fascination for her own, as well as for the "off-islander" who so readily succumbs to her magical appeal.

 Index

A&P supermarket, 126
Academy Hill school, 52
Adams, Alden H., 110
Air New England, 14
Airport, 123
Architecture, 70, 71, 126, 132
Atheneum, the, 65, 73, 88, 92
Automobiles, 119–123
Azores, 37, 41, 58, 59

Bar, the, 58, 63, 70, 83, 85–87, 90, 110, 136
Barnard, Thomas, 21
Beach Street, 87, 121
Beaches, 13, 36, 115, 124, 129, 134
Beard, David O., 68
Beaver (whaler), 48, 49–51
Bedford (whaler), 47
Beinecke, Walter, 132

Bicycles, 14, 132
Block Island, 13, 114
Boat lines, 14
Bonhomme Richard (frigate), 44
Borden, Captain, 90
Bradford Durfee (steamer), 90, 110
Brant Point, 37, 49, 69, 87
Brant Point lighthouse, 37, 39
Broad Street, 52, 64, 87, 132

"Camel," 87
Candlemaking, 52, 69, 84, 91
Capaum Pond, 21, 22, 24, 27, 29, 102
Cape Cod, 14, 31, 32, 104, 128
Cape Horn, 49, 50, 58–59, 65, 92
Cape of Good Hope, 60, 65, 66
Cars, 119–123

Centre Street, 27, 87
Charles W. Morgan (whaler), 50, 51, 59
Chase, Owen, 92–96
Civil War, 84, 85, 91, 105
Club Car, The, 118
Coatue, 126
Cobblestones, 14, 74, 76
Codfish, 24, 102, 104–105, 134
Codfish Park, 100
Coffin, Byron, 135
Coffin, Charles, 77, 80, 81, 83, 105, 114, 116, 117
Coffin, Henry, 77, 80, 81, 83, 105, 114, 116, 117
Coffin, Isaac, 74
Coffin, Jethro, 27
Coffin, Peter, 21
Coffin, Tristram, 20, 21, 27, 31, 74, 135
Coffin, Zenas, 77, 80, 86
Coffin School, 74
Cole, Isaac, 96
Cook's Cycle Shop, 121
"Cord of the Bay," 87
Cuttyhunk Island, 114

Darwin, Charles, 63
Dauphin (ship), 96
Dionis (locomotive), 116
Dionis (beach), 22
Discovery of Nantucket, 17
Drake (ship), 44
Drake, E. L., 91

Eagle (steamer), 107
"Earth oil," 85, 90–91
Elm trees, 77, 80, 81

Essex (whaler), 91–97
Ewer, Peter, 87

Fair Street, 47
Fashions, in early 1800s, 70
Ferries, 122, 128
Fire, Great. *See* Great Fire (1846)
Fisher, Stephen, 68
Folger, Abiah, 72
Folger, Clinton B., 119–122
Folger, Peter, 24, 27, 65, 72, 73, 74
Folly House Hill, 32
Franklin, Benjamin, 24, 72
"Freeze-ups," 108, 109
Fulton, Robert, 107

Galápagos Islands, 63, 92
Gardner, George W., 57
Geary, William H., 87, 88
Gloucester, Massachusetts, 74
Gold Rush (1849), 85, 90
Goose Pond, 116, 118
Gosnold, Bartholomew, 17–18, 83, 134
Grand Banks, 36
Great Fire (1846), 85, 87–90, 110
Great Point, 58, 85
Great Point lighthouse, 39
Greenleaf, Stephen, 21

Haddum, Connecticut, 57
Hamilton (steamer), 107
Haverstick, Iola, 92
Heather, 83, 129
History, early, 17–29, 124
History of Nantucket (Macy), 19
Hither Creek, 18
Hoeg, John, 68
Hooper Farm Road, 116

Houses, 27, 47, 64, 70, 77, 78, 80, 84–85, 87–88, 98, 102, 103, 105, 123, 124, 127, 128, 134
Hummock Pond, 126
Hussey, Christopher, 21, 34, 37, 85
Hussey Street, 70
Hyannis, Massachusetts, 122, 128

India Street, 70, 71
Indian (brig), 96
Indians, 17–18, 19–20, 22–24, 32, 41
Inquirer and Mirror, The, 74, 108, 116
Island Home (steamer), 110

Jared Coffin House, 64
Jethro Coffin House (Oldest House), 25
Jetties beach, 136
Jones, John Paul, 44
Joy, Matthew, 95
Joy, Samuel, 65, 67–68

Liberty Street, 70
Library. *See* Atheneum, the
Lighthouses, 37, 39, 83
Lily Street, 27
"Little Grey Lady of the Sea, The," 13, 136
Location of Nantucket, 13
Lopar, James, 31–32
Low Beach, 117, 118

Macy, Obed, 19, 22, 32, 39, 46, 51, 127
Macy, Richard, 36
Macy, Thomas, 18–24, 27, 31, 36, 37, 39

Macy House, 12
Madaket, 18, 20, 21, 37, 58, 85, 126, 134
Madaket Road, 20, 72
Main Street, 14, 69, 74, 76–77, 80, 83, 87–88, 118, 124, 134
Map of island, 40
Map of town, 113
Marbella, Spain, 101
Marco Bozzaris (steamer), 107
Maria Mitchell house and observatory, 72–74
Martha's Vineyard, 13, 24
Mary Mitchell (whaler), 65–68, 86, 110
Massachusetts (steamer), 110
Mattapoisett, Massachusetts, 57
Maxcy's Pond, 21, 24, 27, 102
Mayhew, Thomas, 21
McCleave, Joseph, Jr., 65–68
Meetinghouse, 27
Melville, Herman, 54
Miacomet, 24
Miacomet Pond, 83
Milestone Road. *See* 'Sconset Road
Mill, first, 24
Mitchell, Maria, 72–74
Mooers, William, 47
Mooers Avenue, 46, 47
Mooers Lane, 47
Mott, Lucretia, 74
Museums, 33, 50, 52, 65

Nantucket, The Far-Away Island (Stevens), 70
Nantucket Historic Commission, 126
Nantucket Inquirer, 74

Nantucket Railroad Company, 116, 118, 119

Nantucket Sound, 21, 22, 27, 30, 44, 70, 108

Nantucket Steamboat Company, 107

Nantucket Surfside Land Company, 114, 117

Naushon (steamer), 111

New Bedford, Massachusetts, 83, 91, 107

Oak (bark), 86

Oldest House, 27

Old Mill, 14, 37, 124

Old North Church, 27, 29

Old South Wharf, 39, 42

Orange Street, 52

"Original Nine Purchasers," 21, 30

Pacific National Bank, 74, 75, 77, 88

Paddock, Ichabod, 32

Peedee Village. *See* Sesachacha Village

Peter Foulger Museum, 65, 130

Pile, William, 21

Pocomo Head, 31, 126

Pollard, George, 92, 94–96

Polpis (Podpis) Road, 103

Prospect Hill, 14, 37, 124

Quakers and Quakerism, 19, 39, 41, 44, 70, 72, 103

Quaise, 21, 102, 106

Quary, Abram, 23

Quidnet, 24, 32, 134

Railroad, 114–119

Ranger (ship), 44

Restaurants, 74, 118, 132

Revolution, 41, 42–47, 104

Rose (ship), 49

Salisbury, Massachusetts, 18, 19, 21, 22, 41

Sankaty, 17, 105, 134

Sankaty Head lighthouse, 82, 83

Saul's Hills, 14, 127

Savage, John, 32

Scallop season, 134

Schools, 52, 74

'Sconset. *See* Siasconset

'Sconset (locomotive), 117

'Sconset Road (Milestone Road), 120–121, 127

Sesachacha Village, 24, 102

Settlers, early, 17–41

Shaw, Marquis, 68

Shepherd, Betty, 92

Sherburne, 21–22, 24, 27, 29, 45, 52, 102

Ship's Inn (restaurant), 74, 132

Shipyard, 49, 57, 69, 116

Siasconset, 17, 24, 98–105, 114, 117, 121, 126

Size of island, 13

Society of Friends. *See* Quakers and Quakerism

Soldiers' and Sailors' monument, 80

Stackpole, Edouard, 92

Starbuck, Edward, 18, 20, 21, 23, 27, 31

Starbuck, George, 80

Starbuck, Joseph, 78, 79, 84

Starbuck, Matthew, 80

Starbuck, William, 80

Steamboat Wharf, 33, 52, 108, 116

Steamers, 90, 107–111, 128

140

Steamship Authority, 13, 121
Stevens, William, 70
Story, Thomas, 41
Story of the Island Steamers, The
    (Turner), 108
Straight Wharf, 35, 36, 42, 70, 122,
    132
Sunset Hill, 27
Surfside, 24, 105, 114, 115, 116,
    117
Swain, John, 21
Swain, M., 68
Swain, Richard, 21

Telegraph (steamer), 107–110
"Three Bricks," (mansions), 79,
    80
Three Brothers (whaler), 78, 85
Tom Nevers Head, 117, 118, 126
Tourism, 98–111, 114, 122–123.
    See also Visitors
Train, 114–119
Trees, 77, 80, 83, 124, 127
Tuckernuck Island, 134
Turner, Harry, 108

Unicorn (brig), 43
Unitarian Church, 52

Vestal Street, 73–74
Visitors, 14, 98–111, 128–130, 132.
    See also Tourism

War of 1812, 54, 104
Weeweeder, 24, 105
Wesco Pond, 24, 27
West Chester Street, 26, 27
West Indies, 46, 57, 58
Whaling, 23, 24, 29, 30–41, 42, 44,
    45–47, 49–52, 54, 55–68, 69, 70,
    74, 76, 78, 83, 84–97, 104, 114,
    132
Whaling Museum, 33, 50, 52, 65,
    87, 130
Widow's walk, 63–64, 77
William, Earl of Sterling, 21
Windmill, 24
Winter, 134
Women, Nantucket, 63–65, 72–74,
    103
Woods Hole, Massachusetts, 68,
    128
Worth, Paul, 49–50
*Wreck of the Whaleship Essex,
    The,* 92

Young's Bicycle Shop, 130

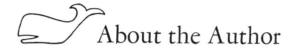 About the Author

WINSTON WILLIAMS was born in New York City and attended the Groton School in Massachusetts and Trinity College, Hartford, Connecticut.

In 1956 he sailed as third mate with Commander Irving Johnson aboard the famous brigantine *Yankee* during her last world cruise. Later, after sailing as first mate on board Sterling Hayden's schooner *Wanderer* in the South Seas, he bought his own 45-foot schooner and sailed from the West Coast to Tahiti in 1960.

While spending a number of years in the Philippines, Mr. Williams wrote numerous articles for the national magazines and newspapers. He has also contributed to *National Geographic*, *Connecticut Magazine*, and *The Inquirer and Mirror*, Nantucket's own newspaper.

He first saw Nantucket as a child, and the island remains his first love. He now lives there permanently where he free-lances as both photographer and writer.